THE LAW OF HYPNOSIS

HOW TO COMMUNICATE WITH THE
HYPNOTIC MIND AND GET EVERYTHING
YOU WANT OUT OF LIFE!

Bryan J. Westra

Indirect Knowledge Limited
MURRAY, KENTUCKY

Copyright © 2014 by Bryan J. Westra.

All rights reserved. No part of this publication may be reproduced, distributed or transmitted in any form or by any means, including photocopying, recording, or other electronic or mechanical methods, without the prior written permission of the publisher, except in the case of brief quotations embodied in critical reviews and certain other noncommercial uses permitted by copyright law. For permission requests, write to the publisher, addressed "Attention: Permissions Coordinator," at the address below.

Bryan James Westra/Indirect Knowledge Limited
2317 University Station
Murray, Kentucky/42071
www.indirectknowledge.com

Book Layout ©2014 Indirect Knowledge Limited

Ordering Information:
Quantity sales. Special discounts are available on quantity purchases by corporations, associations, and others. For details, contact the "Special Sales Department" at the address above.

The Law of Hypnosis/ Bryan Westra. —1st ed.
ISBN 978-0-9899464-9-0

DISCLAIMER:

This book is designed to provide information on hypnosis only. This information is provided and sold with the knowledge that the publisher and author do not offer any legal or other professional advice. In the case of a need for any such expertise consult with the appropriate professional. This book does not contain all information available on the subject. This book has not been created to be specific to any individual's or organizations' situation or needs. Every effort has been made to make this book as accurate as possible. However, there may be typographical and or content errors. Therefore, this book should serve only as a general guide and not as the ultimate source of subject information. This book contains information that might be dated and is intended only to educate and entertain. The author and publisher shall have no liability or responsibility to any person or entity regarding any loss or damage incurred, or alleged to have incurred, directly or indirectly, by the information contained in this book. You hereby agree to be bound by this disclaimer or you may return this book within the guarantee time period for a full refund.

AFFILIATE DISCLOSURE:

In the interest of full disclosure, this book contains affiliate links that might pay the author or publisher a commission upon any purchase from the company. While the author and publisher take no responsibility for the business practices of these companies and or the performance of any product or service, the author or publisher has used the product or service and makes a recommendation in good faith based on that experience.

THE CONTENTS

INTRODUCTION TO NEW TERMINOLOGY AND AN EDUCATION IN THE HYPNOTIC MIND 1

HYPNOSIS 11

    WHY IS HYPNOSIS USEFUL FOR MANIFESTING WHAT YOU WANT IN LIFE? 12

    WHAT IS HYPNOSIS 12

    HOW DO YOU DO HYPNOSIS 16

    WHAT IF YOU UTILIZED HYPNOTIC COMMUNICATION TO GET YOU WHAT YOU WANT 19

    CHAPTER NOTES 22

    ACTION STEPS 23

MANIFESTING 25

    WHY IS MANIFESTING IMPORTANT 26

    WHAT CAN THOUGHT BECOME 28

    HOW CAN YOU MANIFEST WHAT YOU WANT 34

- WHAT IF YOU EXPERIENCE SLOW RESULTS .. 38
  - CHAPTER NOTES 41
  - ACTION STEPS 44
- HEALTH 47
  - WHY IS HEALTH SO IMPORTANT 49
  - WHAT IS GOOD HEALTH 51
  - HOW DO WE STAY HEALTHY 52
  - WHAT IF I DON'T HAVE THE TIME 54
  - CHAPTER NOTES 57
  - ACTION STEPS 59
- BUSINESS 61
  - WHY IS HYPNOSIS IMPORTANT TO USE IN YOUR BUSINESS 64
  - WHAT CAN THE LAW OF HYPNOSIS DO FOR YOUR BUSINESS 67
  - HOW CAN YOUR EMPLOY HYPNOSIS TO GAIN COMPETITIVE ADVANTAGE IN BUSINESS 70

WHAT IF UTILIZING THE LAW OF HYPNOSIS DOES NOT SEEM TO WORK FOR YOUR BUSINESS 72

CHAPTER NOTES 74

ACTION STEPS 76

WEALTH.. 79

WHY HAVE I NOT ACHIEVED FINANCIAL SUCCESS AND SUSTAINED IT................................. 86

WHAT DO I NEED TO KNOW BEFORE I LEARN HOW TO BECOME WEALTHY BY HARNESSING THE LAW OF HYPNOSIS.. 89

HOW TO BECOME WEALTHY USING THE LAW OF HYPNOSIS... 91

WHAT IF I DON'T ATTRACT WEALTH IMMEDIATELY, THEN WHAT 94

CHAPTER NOTES 96

ACTION STEPS 99

RELATIONSHIPS 101

WHY CAN THE LAW OF HYPNOSIS HELP ME MANIFEST MY IDEAL RELATIONSHIP 104

WHAT DO I NEED TO DO TO HYPNOTICALLY ATTRACT THE RIGHT MATE 110

HOW DO I USE THE LAW OF HYPNOSIS TO FALL IN LOVE 116

WHAT IF I WANT TO MANIFEST OTHER TYPES OF RELATIONSHIPS INTO MY LIFE 122

CHAPTER NOTES 124

ACTION STEPS 128

POSTSCRIPT 131

BIBLIOGRAPHY 137

INDEX 141

Dedicated to my Mom—The Great Manifestor!

"What gets in our way is history and culture and religion and economic conditions. It is part of the hypnosis of our social conditioning."

—DEEPAK CHOPRA

CHAPTER 1

INTRODUCTION TO NEW TERMINOLOGY AND AN EDUCATION IN THE HYPNOTIC MIND

Hi my name is Bryan Westra and I want to thank you for your interest in this book. I know you're going to get a tremendous more value from it than what it cost you to purchase it. That being said, I assure you that unless you apply the techniques I'm going to be giving you in this book you can be assured of one thing and that's very simply that you may have wasted your money. Even so, you'll still gain some theoretical benefit in having purchased this book in terms of getting some perspective on the 'Law of Hypnosis' and being able to manifest and bring into your life whatever you need, want, dream, or even can think up for yourself.

I've written this book for the simple reason I cannot hide behind this information any longer. I've read a litany of books on the Law of Attraction. I've read everything from Norman Vincent Peale, Dr. Joseph Murphy, The Secret book's authors—especially most if not all of Dr. Joe Vitale's books—Bob Proctor, and Jack Canfield, Earl Nightingale, James Allen, Napoleon Hill, and many other authors who have written and spoken on the exact same topic I'm going to be teaching you here today. The primary difference, however, is the technique I'll be using to help you access your subconscious mind or unconscious mind in order to get everything you've ever dreamed of out of life; the techniques I'm going to be teaching you are simple, easy; yet, most importantly they're effective—they work!

So if you haven't read anything on Law of Attraction, which would surprise me, what I want you to know about the law of attraction is simply that: "What you think about, you bring about!" "Like attracts like!" and "Thoughts are thing." Essentially these New Thought slogans are the basic premise of Law of Attraction. You see, when you think about something, desiring it, believing you can attract it, you can bring that object of your desire into your external reality from the internal thought reality in which it was born as a seeded idea originally and intentionally. In other words, everything created is first created in the mind; and without being first a planted conceptual idea it would never have come about into your external reality. This is taken to mean that if you want something you first have to see it in your mind, want it, believe you can have it, and expect that it will show up, and it will sooner or later.

Having studied the principles of Law of Attraction, and the literature surrounding it in great detail, and then putting it into practice in my own life; namely, experimenting with different techniques and working in the direction of focused intent to perfect my application of said principles for the purpose of manifesting what I want sooner rather than later, and working mindfully toward the outcome of immediacy, I've finally cracked the code. This is what I'll be teaching you beyond anything else in this book.

Now, before we get at all further into this book I have to share with you some new terminology. There are existing terminology which have become mainstream, but which I do not subscribe to using. Even so, these new terms will continue to make more sense to you as you progress throughout this book, I promise. My intention is not to confuse you with new jargon, but, rather, to put into your awareness a method that in my estimation will make a whole lot more sense to you in the end.

Firstly, let's understand the brain in order to understand the conceptualized mind. The 'mind' is a label used to explain consciousness. Now, people have placed labels such as the 'subconscious mind' or 'unconscious mind' into the mainstream in order to explain 'higher' consciousness that is not consciously rational. For this reason we have two minds. This is interesting, because we also have multiple brains that make up our one brain. We have a brain that was developed evolutionarily first; namely, the 'fight/flight' brain. This brain gets triggered anytime we're caught off guard, shocked, surprised, suddenly worried, etc. The next brain that came about was the limbic system which is the emotional brain. This brain is irrational, non-linear, and not logical. This brain is sometimes referred to as the 'right' brain and it is associated with creative processes, insights, intuition, and instinct. When we're acting on emotion we're usually not consciously critical and for this reason we make decisions (e.g., buying decision) without considering the logical implications. The last brain which developed was the logical rational brain; namely, the cortex. This brain is responsible for structure, sequencing, language, and processes. This brain is the one we use to do critical thinking activities; like following instructions (e.g., step 1., step 2., step 3., etc.) to carryout out an assignment or complete a goal initiative.

As you might guess each of these three brains has a usefulness. The fight/flight brain keeps us safe and able to act quickly and efficiently to avoid dangers. The emotional brain allows us to 'sense' insightfully how we feel about something happening in our lives. The logical brain allows us to act strategically and get things done successfully.

The conscious mind is associated with the logical brain. The unconscious mind is associated with the emotional brain. I believe the reason most people label the minds 'conscious' and 'unconscious' is because the logical brain is perceptive and therefore in use when we're alert and able to perceive reality through our five senses as we go about our day. The 'unconscious' is reflective of the emotional side of our natures that are more abstract linguistically—you can't see 'love' or 'sadness', etc. You might argue you can see tears which are reflective of sadness, however, keep in mind, tears are 'not' an emotion, but, rather, an indicator of an emotion being experienced mentally.

This makes sense on some levels to me as to why people utilize these terms. However, I prefer to use the terms 'mind' to represent the logical rational brain, and the 'hypnotic mind' to represent the 'emotional mind'. Let me explain why:

Many people erringly will say that when we're awake we're conscious; when we're asleep we're unconscious. This isn't actually true. The brain has other conditioned states which show up as 'brain waves' that can be measured with an Electroencephalography (EEG). These brain waves are divided up into bands of speed ranges; measured in hertz per second. A hertz is defined as one cycle per second. These bands represent different areas of the brain where electrical activity is present. Incidentally, each of these bands shows up whenever we are found to be in a certain state of consciousness.

The first state is labeled: BETA. Beta waves range between 16 – 31 hertz. In this state, humans are conscious, attentive, critical thinking, focused, and on high alert. This state is where we're mindful of what's going on around us. For this reason I label this conceptual construct of consciousness as the 'mind'. So 'mind' equals 'mindful'; what is called logical, rational, sensible, critically important, etc.

The second state is labeled: ALPHA. Alpha waves range between 8 – 15 Hz. In this state, humans are relaxed, reflective, and tend to daydream, or focus intently on something (e.g., an object) while mentally being someplace else. This is a state of where rapid eye movement (RIM) happens. These alpha states happen around every 90 – 120 minutes of our waking day. These cycles of transitioning out of beta states and into alpha states are known as ultradian rhythms. The words 'transitioning out' can also be called 'trance-ing out'. Ultradian rhythms represent biological cycles of less than 24 hours per day. In the case with daydreaming and trance-like states these rhythms, as mentioned, recur every 90 – 120 minutes; yet, once in an alpha-state the experience of zoning out, or being in flow, or hyperfocus can last a good 20 minutes or so on average. One way to think of this is to reason it as a rotation between the 'mind' and the 'hypnotic mind'.

The 'hypnotic mind' is the state of mind that happens when we hyperfocus ourselves out of logical consciousness. We may blank out, operating on autopilot; doing the work without being aware we are doing it. You become aware of everything; yet, not aware of anything. This is the hypnotic state. Your 'hypnotic mind' is operating outside of alert consciousness.

So you see, now, why I refer to this mind as the 'hypnotic mind'; namely, because the trance state it represents is the hypnotic state. This 'hypnotic mind' works in pictures, imagination, pretend, and insights. I was taking my dog Foxy Brown for a walk some days ago and I entered this hypnotic state of mind and began imagining a story in my mind as though it were real. Twenty minutes later when I snapped out of that state, returning to the state of mindfulness, I reflected back consciously on what I had been thinking about and tried to make sense of why I was having that experience specifically fantasizing those experiences I was having moments earlier. I realized what had happened and knowing what I know, which I will be teaching you in this book, I was able to conclude that I was communicating directly with my hypnotic mind mentally experiencing some events I have been intentionally working to manifest outwardly into my external reality.

This book is all about creating your own reality; namely, that you might experience this reality though your five senses and perceive it as real as anything else you experience as real. It is not about wishful-thinking, or lying to yourself in hopes of getting what you want out of life; rather, my aim here is to teach you a life-changing system for manifesting your conceptual reality into an actual perceptual reality.

The third state is labeled: THETA. Theta waves range between 4 – 7 Hz. In this state, humans slow down even more than they do while in the alpha state. During this deeper trance-like experience it is common for individuals to experience insights that seem to just come to them. Theta states occur just before falling off to sleep at night and just upon waking up fully in the morning. It is that experience of being half-awake and half-asleep. During this period of time the 'hypnotic mind' is most receptive to suggestions, because the alert 'mind' is not alert enough to reject suggestions.

To contrast this point, and I don't know if you'll be able to relate to this at all, but my partner in crime; that is, my significant other Jennifer will often tell me to do something like take the dog for a walk, or whatever, but whenever she asks me to do this while I'm in this state I find myself mindlessly getting up and getting dressed and taking the dog for a walk. Usually, by the time I get through walking my dog, I'm awake and more functioning. Interestingly enough though I usually come up with some brilliant idea that I just have to write down during this period of waking up fully. In fact, I have a whole desk drawer filled with scrap papers in which are written down these ideas of mine. This book happened to be one of those ideas, incidentally.

The forth state is labeled: DELTA. Delta waves range between 0.1 – 3 Hz. In this state, humans experience delta states as actual sleep. During this period the mind shuts down completely and the human sleeps unconscious of the world outside of sleep. For most of us, we experience between 25 – 35% of our lives asleep, experiencing delta.

So you see, the world we live in is only partly consciously lived; openly, alert consciousness, in which we reason and logic mindfully through life, makes up only a fraction of our way of life.

The last point I want to mention, before we really dive into this book, is the argument many New Thought gurus might use to hide behind whenever somebody buys a book like this one, and *doesn't achieve* the outcomes they desire. The answer is usually something like: "The universe is trying to teach you a lesson," or "An aspect or part of yourself is not on board and because of this you're not able to attract to you what you want," or "If you really 'believed' you'd have what you wanted; you must not really believe."

These are, I should mention, only some of what is said whenever somebody doesn't get the results of following the formula for manifesting something intangible into something tangible. In this way, those who get results (regardless of why) assume why, and those who do not get results (regardless of why) assume why.

This book will teach you a method that works for me and every person who's kept in touch with me whom I have taught this method to. I won't claim your results will be the same, but I believe they will; that is, you'll get what you want if you follow this strategy.

All I ask from you is that you simply suspend your disbelief temporarily and take a leap of faith with me down this new journey.

Every great thing in my life has come about whenever I suspended my disbelief, and took a leap of faith, and had the attitude: "What the heck! Why not? Both the cost and possible loss are miniscule compared to the benefits of what I will receive is my faith leads me where I desire." In this same way I ask that you simply consider that the possible loss is only the cost of this book, and the payoff for purchasing this book is that you live happily ever after like a fairytale princess.

CHAPTER 2

HYPNOSIS

Hypnosis is a very simple process, which involves communicating with your 'hypnotic mind'. This communication takes place by hyperfocusing, subsiding, confusing, or for that matter putting to rest your critical thinking mind.

When you were a child you mother might have lulled you off to sleep at night in her arms. This gentle rocking hypnotized you and eventually you fell asleep. Repetition is a great way for focusing attention and doing exactly the same thing. The 'feeling' of religiousness is the feeling of 'hypnosis'. Hypnosis is an altered state of mind that allows you to do things without having to critically think about doing them.

Many cults and religions use repetitious chants as a means of quieting the mind, focusing attention, helping their members zone-out; in particular, to make then susceptible to explicit and implied suggestions, because through doing these practices they become put under hypnosis—less mindful—less able to critically think for themselves. This experience of 'hypnosis' can be called many things in such groups—for example, communing with God, or becoming one with the universe or nature. It's still hypnosis, however.

WHY IS HYPNOSIS USEFUL FOR MANIFESTING WHAT YOU WANT IN LIFE?

Hypnosis is useful because it is the perfect state of mind to be in to communicate with the 'hypnotic mind'. The hypnotic mind is the starting point for manifesting anything you want in your life.

The hypnotic mind is the field of infinite possibilities. It is where you plant your seeds of intention and desire and then nourish these seeds with mental water until which time your desires become manifested in your outward reality.

In order to bring about your desires all you must do is communicate hypnotically with your hypnotic mind. Communicating hypnotically is a bit different than communicating logically using a structured language. The reason for this is that the 'hypnotic mind' communicates in mental pictures and emotions. Remember it's an emotional mind.

WHAT IS HYPNOSIS

Hypnosis is a state of mind. In this state of mind you sort of escape reality as you perceive it through your five senses to be. In the state of hypnosis you're open minded and able to conceive of anything without the limitations imposed by conscious critical thinking controlled by the critical 'mind'. When anything is possible you're able to possibly do anything.

Think about children: they are impressionable, darling, and brilliantly imaginative. Children play make believe and pretend and in doing so create fantasy worlds in which they thrive. Children don't typically plan; they play. This is something you need to wrap your mind around, because planning can be useful for acting out a sequence; yet, it is also limiting in terms of naturally letting your hypnotic mind carry out a task without you having to plan it out. All you simply do, as children do, is will it hypnotically and intention it.

The will is your conscious desire to do something or have something or experience something. Much of the time we do not know why we want what we want. We often want things because we're conditioned to think that we should aspire to have and achieve certain things throughout our life. It sort of parallels the ultradian rhythms in many ways, only these cycles are more like life cycles. We're born, we experience childhood, we learn what is valuable and worth knowing and having and what is not through other people we learn from or are influenced by, and we continue along the same path of great expectations: (a) get an education, (b) get a good job, (c) get a life partner, (d) have children, (e) save for retirement, (f) retire, and (g) leave a positive mark on society, before we leave this world.

In this way these things are where we align our conscious thoughts. For many of us if we're not living congruently in alignment with these goals we're not living. Dissonance happens whenever we stop for too long and consider how far from the mark we are in terms of achieving the things we think we should be achieving.

Competition is also something that comes about. How much or how less are we succeeding compared to others when it comes to achieving these things society values as importantances? When we find someone else is quickly rising in success whom we consider a peer we may become jealous of their successes. We may become motivated to drive harder and push ourselves in a strictly fashion to do even more than we're doing to achieve the outcomes we believe we have to be achieving.

I want you to ponder over this some in your mind as you read through this book. Think about what's really important to you in terms of your values and ask yourself in what way these things are important. How do these outcomes control your happiness and overall success? Then think back to childhood and deeply assess the people who have influenced your values.

The reason I suggest you do this is because there are five things that are woven together into a matrix which forms your critical faculty. The critical faculty, by the way, is the aspect of yourself that reject or accepts suggestions. This critical faculty is a metaphoric filter that lets in some information and suggestions into your 'hypnotic mind' while denying entry to other information and suggestions.

These five things that make up the critical faculty are: values, beliefs, memories, thinking patterns, and your current state of mind. Let's explore each of these in more detail, because they could be the very thing that stands in the way of you manifesting what you want into your life, and not.

I. Values: Values are what's important to you. Oftentimes what's important is governed by your past experiences and past conditioning of by society and the people you most identify yourself with.

II. Beliefs: Beliefs are what you believe; regardless if it's true or not. It is important to take a look at our beliefs from time to time to assess if they serve us positively or negatively.

III. Memories: Memories are what we recall mentally from our past. Memory has been studied in great measure in the field of psychology and has proven to be not so accurate. What we recall is not always what happened precisely.

IV. Thinking Patterns: Thinking patterns are what we think about most often and habitually. These habitual thoughts have a real influence over our will and what we let happen in our lives. These patterns are often patterns we're not aware of, and what happens is they have a tendency to take over our decision making ability where we make decisions unconsciously instead of consciously. This is one reason when we're being sold something, often we'll outright reject a proposition before the sales person has even had time to tell us what he or she's got for us.

V. Current State: Current state is how you feel and what mood you happen to be in at any given moment. States are contagious—for example, when we spend time in the company of someone depressed we might ourselves become depressed feeling.

HOW DO YOU DO HYPNOSIS

We've talked about how hypnosis is a naturally occurring state that happens every 90 – 120 minutes of our waking day; lasting for approximately 20 minutes, before we recycle back into our conscious alert state. Hypnosis also happens naturally when we're engaged and hyperfocused on something—for example, while we're watching programming on television, or performing a monotonous task such as one an assembly line worker might perform. Hypnosis also is induced with slowed activities, because, and going back to that example of a mother lulling her child to sleep, hypnosis comes about when we're approaching relaxation and restfulness. An example where hypnosis takes place rather covertly is during a boring lecture when the college professor might be talking in a monotone, speaking about 1/3 the rate of a normal rate of speed. This slowed rate and monotone seem to have a hypnotic affect over us causing us to zone out and blank out, and, for many college students, eventually fall asleep.

These techniques I've just outlined can be used to intentionally hypnotize yourself, and even other people covertly. All you simply have to do to hypnotize someone is to slow your speech patterns and start to become hypnotized yourself. Like any state, hypnosis is also contagious.

The actual process by which hypnosis happens is actually a systematic sequence that can be applied both on ourselves (e.g., self-hypnosis) and others. Let's look at that sequence in more details:

I. Focus Attention: The first thing you can do to start the hypnotic process is to focus your attention on a spot on a wall, a candle flame, or for that matter anything that can consume your full attention completely.

II. Bypass the Critical Faculty: We've mentioned that the critical faculty is a matrix of five elements; namely: (a) values, (b) beliefs, (c) memories, (d) thought patterns, and (e) current state of mind. These elements work to assist the critical 'mind' to make sure that some suggestions enter the 'hypnotic mind' while others do not. We generally accept what we 'believe' as worthy of passing through to the 'hypnotic mind'; what we value as worthy and safe for passage; what we remember from the past as being useful as worthy; we want congruity with our thought patterns and thinking or else we may feel like an idea or suggestion isn't worthy for further contemplation; and, lastly, we make a lot of critical decisions based on how we feel and our current state of mind when presented with an idea or suggestion. For these reasons we have to create either a distraction or appeal to someone's values, believes, thinking, and current state of mind if we want to keep their guard down and have them simply accept an idea without outright rejecting it.

III. Stimulate a Hypnotic Response: A hypnotic response can be something repetitive, emotionally charged, and essentially anything that induces a hypnotic trance.

Once in trance the hypnotic subject is hyper suggestible and likely to accept any idea or post hypnotic command as plausible and in this way make it happen to come about. For our purposes we're looking at this from a self-hypnosis perspective and from a perspective based on manifesting thoughts into things.

For example we can hypnotize ourselves very simply by listening to a self-hypnosis audio that has been architected with our specific hypnotic suggestions we want our hypnotic mind to carry out for us. Again, we're not dealing with a critical thinking 'mind'; we're dealing with a 'hypnotic mind' and for this reason you must suspend your disbelief in how this process of manifesting comes about. The process is illogical and won't be believable anyways for most people. It would be the same as me trying to get you to play pretend with me and telling you that our magic make believe world is actually reality. You might look at me funny! So just suspend your disbelief and run with me here.

WHAT IF YOU UTILIZED HYPNOTIC COMMUNICATION TO GET YOU WHAT YOU WANT

You've now been given the instructions for hypnotizing yourself for the purpose of communicating with your 'hypnotic mind'; yet, you still don't know the language by which to get you what you want, do you?

In this section I want to take a brief moment to teach you about the language of the 'hypnotic mind'. A very basic way of conveying the language of the 'hypnotic mind' is to go back to the example of daydreaming where you might be imagining yourself wealthy, youthful, vibrant, and driving around in that expensive new car or walking through the entranceway of that fabulous new mansion. It really doesn't matter what the thoughts are that you have when you do this—it's the point that really matters. You see the hypnotic mind works in pictures and absorbs suggestions presented to it in stories and mental stories. In fact when you watch a movie that sucks you in transports you off to a whole new world, often you're playing scenes from that movie in your head, long after the movie has finished. You're relying on mental pictures which your hypnotic mind fuses together to make those pictures into a movie, and experiencing it as a mental experience.

When you pretend in your mind that you're wealthy and live in a beautiful mansion and have the perfect life you're communicating unintentionally with your 'hypnotic mind'. This communication is going in; however, the aspects of your decision making process aren't always on board with the idea, i.e. your critical faculty.

The idea that you live in a mansion when all you've ever lived in has been a hovel are mismatched in terms of your thought patterns. The idea that you live in a mansion when all you've ever lived in has been a hovel are incongruent with your past memories. The idea that you live in a mansion when all you've ever lived in has been a hovel may counter your values—for example, you may value living simple and modestly and not whatsoever extravagantly. The idea that you live in a mansion when all you've ever lived in has been a hovel may be opposing to your beliefs about the way you will actually live—for example, you may believe that having such a fine home is against God's will for you, or something that will make you worst off for in the end. Interestingly, you may not even know what beliefs are limiting you from living in such a nice new home. The idea that you live in a mansion when all you've ever lived in has been a hovel could very well be offensive to considering your current state—for example, maybe you're in a state of mind that is worried about just getting this month's bills paid, and the idea of living in a mansion may be a 'ridiculous' fantasy.

Often there are more than one of the five that are shooting down ideas and preventing us from communicating what we want with our 'hypnotic mind'. That is, we may not believe that a mansion is going to show up in our reality because we can't seem to get enough money up together now to merely pay our bills, and it could be a belief that in order to live in a mansion we must pay for it, and further more we may think in terms of value that this money would surely be better spent on something else besides a mansion could come into the picture for us.

One of the techniques that people have used to manifest what they want has been 'vision boards'; namely, cork boards where individuals have pinned up pictures cut from magazines or collected from online and made a type of mirage of what they want to manifest into their lives. There have been many reported instances where an individual will have put these board into a box, or attic, only to years later find them and learn that they are living in the same type of home, driving the same type of car, and doing the same types of activities that they had years earlier dreamt of doing.

There's value in understanding this technique. There's value because it tells us insightfully how the 'hypnotic mind' can be communicated with; explicitly, with pictures, thoughts, and feelings. Tied together these three elements are the language of hypnosis. This is why a stage hypnotist can have someone believing that they are actually riding a duck. They induce hypnosis, then instruct in pictures, creating an exciting state of riding a duck, and make the subject actually feel like it is possible. To the hypnotized subject they are not hypnotized; they're riding a duck, having a wonderful time doing so.

CHAPTER NOTES

In this chapter you leant about hypnosis—why it's important, what it is, how to hypnotize yourself and others, and in what way you can utilize hypnosis in order to communicate with your hypnotic mind.

I explained to you that hypnosis is important because it is the state necessary to communicate hypnotically with the hypnotic mind. When you do you're able to communicate in a way that limits your conscious mind's influence over your beliefs, values, thoughts, memories, and current state of mind.

I also explained what hypnosis is: It is a state that can happen naturally or intentionally on purpose in which we take ourselves out of our logical rational state from which critical thinking is performed and transition over to the 'hypnotic state' where anything is possible and able to be imagined as true.

I further taught you the hypnotic process: (a) focus attention, (b) bypass the critical faculty, and (c) stimulate the hypnotic mind through stimulating a hypnotic response (e.g., emotional response). Once achieved you're brain waves have altered and gone from a 'beta state' to an 'alpha state'. Once in this state you can receive hypnotic suggestions by delivering them to yourself in the form of mental pictures, feelings, and thoughts. Communicating in this way ensures your seeds of desire are planted and only now need to be hypnotically watered. By the way, 'water' is often a symbol for the 'unconscious' or 'hypnotic mind'.

ACTION STEPS

The following action steps are meant to help you think about what you want, to bring about what you think. Please do the exercises even if you've done them before in the past on some other course. Your compliance is evidence of your real desire to manifest outwardly what you most seek, desire, and dream of having, experiencing, and achieving in life.

I. Make a list of what you want to manifest. Do not worry about how absurd it sounds or seems. Find pictures to represent what you want and create a visual kaleidoscope which you will see every single day. Keep it posted there and don't take it down until you achieve your gain.

II. Make a habit of several times a day hypnotizing yourself. It could be that you stare off into oblivion while looking intently at a spot on your wall until which time you fall under the spell of hypnosis. While under hypnosis mentally picture your desired outcome as completed, feeling how you would feel, and thinking how you would think. This is called future pacing experiences, and will help you 'communicate hypnotically' with your 'hypnotic mind'. This is very simple to do and doesn't take much time. Do it regularly and frequently though.

III. Journal your hypnotic experiences and elaborate in this 'hypnotic journal' everyday about the subtle shifts happening in your thinking, your values, your beliefs, your past memories and how you may be looking at them differently than before, and note down your current state of mind, i.e., how you feel. Do you best to write in your 'hypnotic journal' at the same time every day. Make sure you do this while you're still under hypnosis in order to express yourself hypnotically in this journal. You want your 'hypnotic mind' communicating back to you. This feedback is important, because when you're conscious again and reading your daily entry you'll become more aware of how much more in sync you are with your 'hypnotic mind' than you might have been the day before.

CHAPTER 3

MANIFESTING

Manifesting has become a type of buzz word since the book *The Secret* has come out and other Law of Attraction books, programs, and products. This word cuts to the chase surrounding the 'essence' of law of attraction; namely, in that it defines the act of an outcome coming about.

Manifesting is a presupposition that assumes something will come about through the act of manifesting. This is an interesting way of looking at this term in my opinion. There's no room for failure—only success. What you want you will get through the act of manifesting. It also seems implied that by not manifesting one will achieve anything besides the desired outcome.

It may be noteworthy to consider how all the possibilities of various outcomes which could by chance come about imply indirectly that when some desired outcome comes about to fruition it would seem without question that it was due to the act of manifesting, and not any other cause besides. I'll let you debate that quietly to yourself if you wish to. I do not.

Assuming then that manifesting is an act of doing something, it must be then that in order to achieve an outcome one desires one must act. Some might argue that the act of not acting is still an act, but I won't delve into that discussion.

For you, I want the outcomes to come about that you desire. Throughout this book in future chapters we'll look at some generalized categories that seem to be of importance to a majority of society. In this chapter though I want to look at the action steps thought to bring about a result.

WHY IS MANIFESTING IMPORTANT

Manifesting is important because it starts somewhere and ends somewhere else. It is a process that can be observed as a logical model.

Where exactly does manifesting begin? To start is begins as a thought. This thought is similar to the hope that a young person has about their future. There's uncertainty in it. There's mystery. There's intrigue. There's a story beginning but no clue about how the end will result.

Like most stories, in youth, we believe somewhere that the end will be a happy ending. This is a great start, because the outcome is believed to be a positive one.

Manifesting begins with an imaginary thought that holds infinite possibilities. An inquiry into the nature of thought has brought be as far back as India's rich Vedic history; specifically, to a Sanskrit text named: Sri Lalita Sahasranama. I have studied this text, memorized it, obsessed over its hidden meanings, and, done, much like that of a literary theorist who lives to understand the essence as well as every coded message in one of the classics contained in the cannon of literary greatness.

One day, and I have to share this short story with you, I was hypnotized from chanting these 1000 Sanskrit mantras, which make up the Lalita Sahasranama, and I gained a spiritual or hypnotic insight. I came to realize that the Sanskrit word 'chitta' which equates to 'memory' in English, yet, a deeper understanding of the word leads one to conceive of a better synonym, which might equated to the 'hypnotic mind'. The word 'chitta' means 'mind stuff' which comprise the invisible intangible substances that that defy the laws of material existence.

Not really though. You see this 'chitta' or 'stuff' are invisible impressions located in the 'hypnotic mind' and which can be recalled as memories, imaginings, ideas, concepts, and so on. Most people would argue that if you can observe or experience something you'll likely believe it to be true. If this is the case most people I would imagine reading this book would agree then that the impressions in the mind that they can make or recall from memory, i.e. thoughts, are as real as anything tangible that they might observe with their eyes or hear with their ears. After all the ability to simply stop reading this book and imagine a giraffe in your mind, did then, actually just happen, did it not? If so, isn't this 'real' by definition? It was a real experience you just had, was it not?

So this is as far back as my research takes me in terms of gaining a perspective of when people started understanding the mind, and its functions, even long before science was able to measure brain waves. The 'hypnotic mind' was known about back then, some 5000 years ago. It was known that what you think about, you bring about. It was cautioned that one should be careful of one's thoughts. It was assumed that if you think 'bad' thoughts, bad things happen; likewise, if you think 'good' thoughts, good things happen. How simply amazing!

So now you understand why manifesting is so important, because it has to do with taking this 'chitta' or 'invisible stuff' and from it growing a desired outcome. What is achieved in the end is said to be 'manifested'.

WHAT CAN THOUGHT BECOME

Thoughts can become any tangible or perceivably 'real' outcome, but they can also remain as never more than thoughts, as well. It all really just depends. And, "Depends on what?" you ask me or at least wonder to yourself. Let me explain.

When you or someone you know seems to always be sickly, and you hear other people in their inner circle continually reiterating this as a fact, it is because they are stating the obvious, i.e. the person is always sick it seems. The person sick, or perhaps yourself, comments both internally (self-talk) and externally of this fact. It is believed by you or them, and the sickness continues to support the thought patterns, belief, past recalls of sickness, and the 'sick' state that you or the person sickly finds themselves in. The more obviously sick the sick person is, the more likely the sickness will continue.

A person who constantly worries about never having enough money, or worried that they aren't 'getting ahead' has similar patterns as the sick person. They are constantly thinking about not having enough money or running out of money that they have formed certain habitual thought patterns. These thought patterns and their lack of money help them form certain beliefs; namely, beliefs that tell them they will never have enough. They think about past situations from memories they've gathered about situations where they didn't have enough money and the worry. They might get to a point where they actually start to devalue money and believe that there are other more important things in life than money, to the extent that they actually, secretly, deep down inside themselves, start to dislike money. Their state of mind is one of worry and frustration over being able to afford the life they desire, but don't think they can afford.

Then there're the business people who graduate from top MBA schools, who fear their learnings weren't enough to rise to the top of the corporate ladder. They view others as more worth adversaries that will likely outperform and rise to the top quicker. They start to nurse such thoughts until they become the 'hypnotic focus' in which they start to form recurring thought patterns. Half the time these business professionals aren't even aware they're having these thoughts and concerns. Over time these thoughts become beliefs. The outcomes visible to the business person starts to have them devalue their own ideas about business, causing them to form certain judgments (e.g., businesses take advantage of workers, etc.). In time the person's attitude at work changes and they engage in certain states that aren't conducive for success. They start to reflect on their past and realize that they're fears and worries were spot on from the beginning as they've yet to achieve a measure of success they might have one time envisioned when back in business school. The outcomes of these thoughts become their realities—they remain inferior to others they perceive as superior to them.

Perhaps one of the most saddening situations is what happens when someone in a relationship perceives the other person as outside what they deserve. They might see their partner as deserving of someone better. They might think they deserve someone of a lesser standard. These types of thoughts are a virus that forms patterns that will quickly kill a relationship. The idea that people need to be nicely matched up with people like themselves is a belief based on values that are decided by society, families, and peers. You've heard someone say of someone who has started a relationship with someone 'model-looking', "You lucky person." Inferring that the person is in a relationship with someone above what they are deserving of. These types of statements feed the inner-thoughts of the person and overtime the thoughts become belief and it actually starts to inhibit the person relationally. Eventually, the relationship dies, and it's back to being single.

Other relationships are murdered in the same fashion. These could be work relationships where someone perceives someone 'out to get them' and 'sabotage' their job. This may form as an idea simply from the other person's unwillingness to communicate openly with the person. Lack of communication makes it so that the person starts to fill-in-the-blanks with his or her own ideas about the person; generalizing and distorting what is actually the case (e.g., the person could simply be an introverted personality type). These thoughts continue until they form patterns that repeat at the hypnotic level, and in time become beliefs. Over some time the recall of days past where the other person said the wrong thing or looked at them a certain way, leads them to form judgments and opinions about the person's motivations and intent. In time, what happens, is the person hallucinating these thoughts and ideas which have become, now, beliefs does something to sabotage the working relationship—a relationship that might have actually become a true business friendship.

There are numerous contexts in which individuals rely too heavily on their thoughts, values, beliefs, recollections and current state of mind when it comes to making a decision. It is important to understand that these are all things that make up your critical faculty and which when information is allowed to pass through and into your 'hypnotic mind' are planted as impressions that in time will manifest outwardly into your external reality.

I've mentioned some negative examples here you might relate with. Let me mention a positive one to contrast what thoughts can become—to inspire you with hope.

Perhaps we've all known someone who falls on his or her luck and goes through some devastating time; however, from which goes on to become incredibly successful in business, their relationships, and even become wealthy. These people we might say 'deserve' what they have achieved, because they've gone through so much early on in their lives. In society we value the overcomer, i.e. the underdog who rises to greatness. We believe they 'deserve' their success, because our thought patterns over time have led us to believe this belief. Our memories, when we recall times of people we've known or heard about withstanding trial after trial to eventually master life and gain the object of their desire is quite an empowering memory. It gives us hope that we'll be able to do the same.

So with all these opposing and supporting beliefs, values, memories, thought patterns, and states of mind we find ourselves in, why does it seem near impossible to wish inside your mind, hoping and hoping, and pretending to believe until which time you actually convince yourself that you do believe that you'll achieve what you want to manifest, do people still not acquire externally what they believe they've impressed into their 'hypnotic mind'? This is a good question. Let's answer it.

Let me give you a metaphor that I think you'll understand. Imagine a battlefield. There are two sides. On one side are the 'good guys' and on the other side are the 'bad guys'. This war has been going on for years. When one side has an advantage they end up winning a victory; however, just when they begin celebrating their win, the other side gains an advantage and gains a victory over them as well. This war has no end in sight, because both sides are forces to be contended with.

This is much the same thing that happens inside our own minds. There're two sides. One side is formed by limiting beliefs, values, thought-patterns, memories, and negative states of mind. The other side is formed by encouraging beliefs, values, thought-patterns, memories, and positive states of mind.

You see, sometimes it seems like whenever we achieve a victory or a leg-up that aligns with what our heart wants something comes along to sabotage our successes and bring us down. This conflict which we perceive outwardly in our external environment is caused by our internal conflict dueling it out on the battle field of our minds. It's a constant struggle that wears us down psychologically, and creates a real dilemma when it comes to us getting what we want.

Some people, and you might know of a few right-off, get to a point where they become comfortable with being uncomfortable. They've given up on the idea that their ship will one day come in. They've built walls around their mind (metaphorically) to protect them from outside forces coming in. These are the people who reject ideas that could help them right away, because they've gotten to a point where what they've wanted seems too painful to pursue any longer—they'd rather be left alone to live out their days with as less stress as possible—comfortable with simply existing. Another example of what thoughts can become.

HOW CAN YOU MANIFEST WHAT YOU WANT

In order to manifest your needs, desires, and dreams you need to dissociate yourself from the battlefield and observe what's going on objectively. What this does is allow you to get clarity on what thoughts, beliefs, values, memories, and states of mind are helping you to lose the battle to achieve and receive what it is you really want.

For most people these are limiting beliefs and thought patterns, memories that we can't let go of (e.g., death of a dear loved one, past experience that is blocking us from achieving, etc.), values that do not align with prosperity and success, and states of mind that leave us feeling inadequate, inferior, less deserving, less likely, depressed, and a victim, which all hinder our 'hypnotic mind' from growing our positive thoughts and intentions, which are imprinted in the 'hypnotic mind', but rotting in the ground of defeat, due to heavy flooding of negative thoughts, and lack of positive thoughts and feeling shining down to help the desire seeds to grow. You get the picture of now of what's going on, don't you?

How can you get rid of the hindrances to your manifesting so that these desire seeds can grow and flourish and bring you lasting success, wealth, health, and relationships? Another good question. The answer is hypnosis.

You see when you are hypnotized you're not thinking critically as you do most often throughout your day. Your critical thinking is reactionary thinking that stimulates more of what it sees before it. You don't want more of the same do you? Well, perhaps in some areas of your life you do; however, using hypnosis you can immediately erase the obstacles to your success in manifesting what you want –and, 'get what you want'!

The first step, is to, like I mentioned a moment ago, dissociate yourself emotionally from the warring sides keeping you in conflict with your ability to have what it is you want. Identify what exactly the forces are holding you back. Are they certain values you hold that hurt you from progressing? Are they certain beliefs causing you problems? Are they painful memories you can't let go of? Are they thought patterns you cannot get out of your head? Is it your state of mind? For most of us it is a combination of problem areas in each area. We all have skeletons in our closet we don't want to clean out. We all have values that we think are important to us, yet which actually are hurting us from positive growth. We all have thoughts that plague our minds—unless we're a Hindu swami engaged in absolute detachment from everything life has to offer potentially—in which case this book probably can't help you. We all have states of mind that seem to define our personality, but also cause us to think certain things about ourselves, making up a false identity that we believe is true about ourselves.

These things have to be dealt with first. It is important. It is psychologically challenging to do for some of us. It requires us to re-open our minds back up to where they might have been when we were precious innocent children enjoying life day-by-day while entertaining ourselves with our inspired imaginations.

Think about it. You have a lifetime of values, thoughts, beliefs, memories from your past experiences, and a state of mind that is defined by all these things. Of course not always are we in the same state of mind, but look at where you state usually is by comparison of where it's not always, yet only to the extent you can you're not as positive as you could be.

After taking an inventory of all this about yourself the next step is to learn to control your mind. For most people the mind has control of them.

> *"For him who has conquered the mind, the mind is the best of friends; but for one who has failed to do so, his very mind will be the greatest enemy."*—Bhagavad Gita 6:6

How do you control your mind, however? This isn't as difficult as it may at first seem. What you do is make time to prioritize what you want out of life. Then you take an objective assessment of what is required to get it. This of course means what mind set is necessary, what thought patterns are most conducive, what memories are most useful for reflecting on, what beliefs will be most advantageous, and what state of mind most beneficial. Once you have achieved writing down these things you'll need to start to frame them in the context of your daily routine. This is where action comes into play.

You'll ask yourself if it is wise to make a time each day to reflect on what you're grateful for, what's been a constant aid in your life that has gotten you the successes you've achieved up to this point, and determine if you need to meditate, do yoga, or begin taking steps in the 'right' direction to start to form an atmosphere through which your right beliefs, right thought patterns, right values, right memories, and right state of mind will be able to harvest the seeds you've impressed into your 'hypnotic mind'.

Whenever a circumstance arises that is in conflict with and incongruent with this new way of being you'll take observation of it in a dissociative state of mind. You'll then remember what behaviors and thoughts are necessary to realign yourself mentally back onto your goals.

You'll want to start taking notice of times when you enter natural hypnosis, noting and then writing down all the thoughts, hallucinations, and mental movies that play out. This will tell you a lot as far as how well you're doing in properly programming your hypnotic mind to manifest what you desire or not—for example, if you mental movie is one that is aligned with what you want, i.e. you're seeing yourself living in that dream home, driving that dream car, enjoying those dream relationships, etc., then you know you're well aligned. However, if you find that your mental movies reflect those old beliefs, worries, fears, inhibitions, that prevent your from moving forward and achieving what you want to manifest, you'll know you have some work to do on yourself. The work, by the way, is simply utilizing self-hypnosis, to implant more positively aligned hypnotic suggestions into your 'hypnotic mind'.

This can be a process. Depending on how conditioned you are to outside stimuli, past experiences, old beliefs, values that aren't really as important as you think they are, and states of mind that hinder instead of help you, will determine how quickly you are able to manifest a new 'reality' into your external existence.

Don't be surprised how quickly you find yourself manifesting certain new events and experiences that reflect a step in the right direction. It's sort of like the vegetable gardener who walks outside the next morning to find that her or his tomato plants have begun producing tiny green tomatoes. Or a squash or zucchini plant has flourished with many small vegetables. It sort of comes as a pleasant surprise to alert you that you're doing a good job gardening and doing what needs to be done to produce healthy plants and therefore healthy fruits and vegetables.

In the same way you'll notice a series of surprising happenings start to take effect from the mental manifesting work that you've been nurturing.

WHAT IF YOU EXPERIENCE SLOW RESULTS

Slow results happen when the battle field has two forces warring against each other. What you want to ideally achieve is an inner peacefulness with yourself. One where only one side exists; that is, where you're whole and complete and all the aspects of yourself are on board with the direction you want to see yourself having accomplished.

This brings me to another point: You want to impress your desired outcomes as having already come about. You want to see the end result as already having happened. You see the problem with memories are that they are in the past. The past, for people, is something certain and real, because its already happened. People hold onto the past for the reason that it feels safe and secure to do so. What's worked in the past is thought to be able to work for a person in the future. A past experience is thought to produce the same outcomes when repeated at a future date. It makes logical sense as it's all about process orientation and it's something the logical 'mind' can get behind and act to achieve. Be cautious, however, because what's worked in the past is not guaranteed to work in future situations necessarily, and what's even more important to consider is that there are 'other', perhaps more advantageous, means to accomplish something. So don't get caught up in the past and assume the thought pattern that what's worked for me in the past is the best solution for me now.

On the other hand, the future is sometimes scary for people to face. This scariness stems from the unknown. If you find yourself afraid of the future and insecure, keep in mind that these types of thought patterns and states of mind will hinder you achieving what it is you desire to manifest.

My recommendation for these issues related to 'time' is to remain in the present, assuming the future that you envision for yourself is already now taking place. You don't have to be worried about what you already know is 'now' taking place. There's a certainty that happens living in the now has that is ideal for manifesting what you desire. Each moment, each day, you'll start to see your outer world reflect your inner desires. The reason for this is that your 'hypnotic mind' is naturally growing into existence the 'chitta' or 'thought stuff' into visible reality for you to see, experience, and know as 'real'.

Many people believe that it is wisest to manifest small things into their existence first, because this breeds and multiplies more faith in the 'hypnotic mind's' power to miraculously bring about larger and larger outcomes that are desired. It really doesn't matter in my opinion, however, I must admit that at first this was my way of learning to trust my 'hypnotic mind'.

What's fascinating, I I'd like to share this story with you, is how I knew other people who believed in the law, which were great manifestors. When I first learned of the law of hypnosis I had peers who were learning at the same time as I was. I have to admit that many of them were wonderful in what they were able to manifest, whereas at first, I was experiencing only small results. This caused me, at the time, to be a little envious and jealous of these peers, which hurt my ability to manifest more positive outcomes I desired. I want to warn you that jealousy, anger, fear, envy, and all these types of thoughts and states of being in are detrimental to your harvest. It's like spraying weed killer on newly grown Bermuda grass landscape—it kills the grass!

You want to learn, and I think it does take learning and practice, to be happy and enthusiastic for other people when they achieve a measure of success. You must be happy for the success of others, realizing that there's enough money, health, happy relationships, success, and more of everything to go around to every human being on the planet. Always keep a happiness for others and what they achieve and succeed in accomplishing. Like attracts like. What you see in others is what is happening to you. When you see other people prospering this is the sign that you are prospering too; even if you don't know it. This was a big lesson I learnt the hard way…I hope to save you from this lesson.

So just remember, slow results, or seeing results that others are having, means that you simply need to reassess your thought patterns, beliefs, values, states, and what you're thinking on from your past. Make sure you don't get frustrated or anxious or start to disbelieve the way manifesting works. Just know it works, and keep an eye out for the signs others around you are prospering, etc., because what you focus on you get more of.

CHAPTER NOTES

In this chapter we covered the importance of manifesting your needs, desires, and dreams. We looked into and investigated how the process of manifesting is more important to focus on than the actual external results produced. When you understand the importance of how the 'hypnotic mind' works to get you what you want, you realize that your actions will take effect as a result, and in return get you what you want. Not understanding how the 'hypnotic mind' works is like starting a business without knowing how your business operates. Without an understanding of how certain actions produce certain results it is like the blind, leading the blind. You continue to act hoping you'll somehow get it right, and be able to achieve what you want. The 'hypnotic mind' works irrespective of how nice a person you are, what your background is, how you see the world, what you believe to be true, or what you value. It simply acts to harvest the seeds you've impregnated it with, when certain conditions are met.

We look also in this chapter at what thoughts can become. We explored what ancient Hindu culture described as 'chitta' or 'thought matter'; that is, we learnt how thoughts are actually invisible matter that forms according to the harvests of the 'hypnotic mind'.

A great way to understand 'thought' is to perceive them as physical invisible matter that comprises everything tangible in the universe. These thought elements are built into existence by the 'hypnotic mind'. When you understand this you'll start to understand that everything you can see, hear, taste, touch, and smell was once just an idea, i.e. thought, in someone's mind, before in time it became made manifest. Nothing gets created without first being a thought.

The next thing we investigated was the process through which we, ourselves, could manifest what we want. This process starts with delving deep within our own psychologies and exploring our own persuasions about what we believe, value, think, remember, and consistently feel about ourselves. From here the instructions get easy, as clarity is discovered, and all that remains is that we eschew the beliefs, values, thinking, past recollections, and states of mind that aren't no longer useful for our reaching what we want out of life. Once we begin to take ourselves out of the picture, dissociating ourselves from our current perceived reality, and allow ourselves an objective look at what is useful to believe, think, value, remember, and feel, then we can start to experience life in a whole new way—a way that is beneficial for getting us what we want.

Lastly, I shared with you a phenomenon that seems to happen to many people when they begin on the journey of manifesting their needs, desires, and dreams; namely, what happens if you perceive achieving the experiences and things you wish to possess as a slow experience. I shared my personal experience of envy, jealousy and judgment on others able to get what they want more quickly than me. I elaborated on why it is important to express and feel joy and happiness for others when they receive and achieve their manifested outcomes, because it is a sure sign that you're on the right path, because like attracts like. What they are experiencing and you're observing is a reflection of what's soon about to happen to you.

ACTION STEPS

The following action steps are meant to help you think about what you want, to bring about what you think. Please do the exercises even if you've done them before in the past on some other course. Your compliance is evidence of your real desire to manifest outwardly what you most seek, desire, and dream of having, experiencing, and achieving in life.

I. Make a list of any thoughts you have while experiencing natural hypnotic phenomenon each day for a week, as best you can. At the end of the week divide these thoughts into positive and negative thoughts. Reflect on the past week when you had these different thoughts and now substitute in positive thoughts where the negatives ones once were.

II. Journal in your 'Hypnotic Journal' all experiences or observances that seem to be bringing you your desired outcome. Then shut your eyes and be grateful that your 'hypnotic mind' is bringing to fruition these things and experiences.

III. Take notes on how people around you are responding and seeming. Are they starting to reflect a positive attitude, starting to get closer to attaining what they most desire? Are you starting to see some of the negative people in your life start to go by the way side? It is important to not be attached to the people, habits, jobs, etc. that keep you from having what you are desiring to manifest. Be grateful for the changes and wish positive things to happen onto others no longer a part of your life. Remember…like attracts like, and not everybody will be of the same vibrational frequency as you now.

CHAPTER 4

HEALTH

I want to start with health because without it nothing else seems to be quite so enjoyable; that is, in terms of what you acquire and succeed at experiencing. Good health seems to augment everybody's life experience. Health is something that you should seek to manifest in great abundance. A lot of our lives spent maybe not so conscious of our health. We have an innate belief, many of us, that health is something we should concern ourselves with later in life. Some of us on the other hand take a proactive role in achieving health throughout our lives through regular exercise, fitness, yoga, meditation, and so on.

Thought this is a positive behavior that stimulates proper health measures while serving to prevent future health problems, it can also have adverse effects that we're not even consciously aware of—for example, if we're focused on being healthy so that we won't become unhealthy, thus fearing unhealthiness, as a possibility, we could be manifesting what it is we don't want into our lives, simply because of our thought patterns and our beliefs, and what we have experienced in the past through other peoples' experiences whom we've known.

So don't get overly caught up on preventing something bad from happening from you, because the very act of doing so could be the very seed thought that manifests to you what you don't want. It's the expectation that if we don't do something that something else will happen, or that if we do happen to do something that something will result that can bind us and hold us captive in our own thinking. As a result the behavior and the outcomes that spawn as a result maybe exactly what we receive. So for this reason my suggestion, and keep in mind this is only an opinion, my opinion, and you'll have to use your own critical mind to decide if this is right and 'useful' for you to believe or not; however, my opinion is that we should keep good health and engage in healthy activities for the purpose of being able to manifest into our lives what it is we desire and wish to acquire. Health in this regard is used for our enjoyment and our ongoing habit of continuing to manifest into our lives what it is we desire on and ongoing basis throughout our lifetime. Consequently, look at health as something that will, 'if I don't stay healthy I will become ill, sick, or acquire a disease or inability to continue living, and so on'; rather, think instead that health is a state of being that is useful for continued manifesting throughout our lives, which makes it possible for us to create different life experiences on an ongoing basis.

WHY IS HEALTH SO IMPORTANT

As I've indicated health is important for a number of reasons: the most important being that you want to be able to maintain a state of mind that is conducive for hypnotically manifesting your needs, desires, and dreams. This is solely the idea that I have.

Now the other thing is important to take note of mentally, regarding why health is so important is how it's important to be able to enjoy, in a healthy capacity, the experiences that you are manifesting and coming into realization of. If we're going to manifest wealth and abundance in our life we want to likewise be able to enjoy what that wealth and abundance can do for us while we're living this human experience.

If we're growing a business and we're focused on business success we want to remain healthy enough to be able to tackle the issues we become confronted with in business. Note, when I use the word 'tackle' I'm not using it in a perverse way to suggest that running a business or growing a business requires any difficulty whatsoever. I'm simply using it as a reference point that many people will be able to identify with who have started businesses in terms of achieving one result in order that they might achieve another result, and continue to grow their business one goal at a time.

Why health is important is that it keeps you healthy in your mindset for continued manifestation for things that you want, desire, and would like to experience in your life so that you can experience them in an enjoyable and pleasurable way which will lead to greater states of excitement, pleasure, and happiness, which are useful states for continuing to manifest the things in life you want.

What can happen sometimes when I comes to health is a condition can occur in a person's life and this condition can be ignored from the viewpoint of the manifestor. When a condition is ignored sometimes we have beliefs and thought patterns, and idea that form inside us that seem to suggest mentally that a condition gone unchecked will lead to a worst health condition later on.

I've seen this very thing happen before in people where they ignore possible health concerns and because of this ignorance these types of health concerns escalate to in kind cause them more grief until which time they become bigger problems. At this point you can be sure that the individual's state of mind will have likely changed and have led to an adverse manifestation of something they don't want happening in their life.

Whenever you experience a condition and a belief or thought pops in that has you believing you are in trouble health wise somehow and in some way what I suggest is you clear your mind and objectively assess how you feel, what you state of mind is, what your beliefs are and from that point make a decision as to how to proceed next. Of course, as a disclaimer here, I am no medical doctor or health professional. I'm not licensed to give you health advice or prescribe you what to do whereas your health is concerned. My advice is that whenever you think, believe, or feel as though you should see a doctor, that you do so.

Again, keep in mind, this is only my opinion. I don't expect you to agree with my point of view on everything, only so far as it's useful for you to do so.

WHAT IS GOOD HEALTH

Good health is not only a physical wellbeing or condition, but it is also a mental state. When you are focused on positive health and feeling good and exuberant about your life experience as it plays out in front of you day-by-day then you tend to do things that promote better health. What I'm suggesting is embark on exercises for your body and exercises for your mind that will promote a positive wellbeing that will allow you to have clarity over your life so that you can make decisions that will positively affect you whether it will be through a yoga regiment, a daily meditation, physical exercises, taking nature walks, walking your dog, playing with your children, or stretching when you get up out of bed in the morning, or whatever the case might be in which you acquire some exercise to nourish your body and mind.

A form of activity on your part pertaining to physical activity can also have an effect on your mental well-being, as well. For this reason it is important to maintain a healthy mind and also a healthy body, because the two work together to keep you happy, healthy, and well.

HOW DO WE STAY HEALTHY

Staying healthy means being consciously aware that to promote a positive existence you should want to promote activities that prompt a healthy lifestyle. Now, this is a presupposition that I'm making; in other words, I'm making the assumption that in order to be healthy a person has to engage in healthy activities. The reason I'm making this presupposition is because it's a presupposition that most people since youth have experienced as a truism. The conditioning of this presupposition is useful in that capacity, as it does not harm our abilities to manifest things into your life; yet, rather, it helps in the manifestation process.

When we exercise our bodies this can be very hypnotic as far at the experience goes. A runner for example can get into the 'zone' as they're repetitiously putting one foot in front of another, the next foot in front of the other, the next foot in front of the other, and this repetition is very hypnotic. As a result it is not uncommon for runners to disengage from their body's activity, in terms of the 'run' itself, and instead focus more internally on other thoughts going through their mind. These thought patterns can be very useful as the runner tends to leave the beta state to enter the alpha state; this alpha state is the hypnotic state that we intentionally put ourselves under while we run in order to gain clarity and insight into our life and the things we want to bring about for ourselves—the actions that we're likely to take—what decisions we should make, and so on and so forth. This is a positive way of making decisions especially when the mind is aligned with hypnotic principles and the Law of Hypnosis. Knowing the Law of Hypnosis simply by entering this state and having our thoughts align with our desires more ensure a positive outcomes results regarding what we want to see manifested in our lives.

Swimming is another activity that is very hypnotic. Lap by lap the swimmer swims; constantly disengaging from the physical body and into the mind. For this reason, swimming is a mental exercise as well as a physical exercise. This brings me to another point and that is sometimes we get caught up in this idea that we should engage in mental activity to manifest things into our life; rather, forgoing exercise and external activities that promote positive health and well-being, which increase our life-force.

This is not necessarily true I would suggest to you, because activities like running, swimming, yoga, and many exercise that strengthen the body's wellbeing are actually also exercises of the mind. The yogi who practices regular yoga engages in various postures while working to clear the mind of negative thoughts and emotions to embark on a transcendental, peaceful, and restful state of being.

Martial arts happens to be another exercise of the body and the mind. Fighting is a mental art. In order to win against an opponent it is important to outthink and out maneuver one's opponent, as much as it is to physically dominate them. As we see with the biblical account of David and Goliath; Goliath was a giant while David was a mere boy. Yet, David with his childlike inventiveness and fearlessness was able to defeat the giant Goliath.

Goliath overestimated his power and abilities just like the hare did in the child's fable of the *Tortoise and the Hare*. The tortoise won the race due to the hare's overestimation that he had no way but to win the race against a slow turtle.

My advice to you is to incorporate some type of physical activity into your life that will promote not only physical well-being, but also mental well-being. This can be done at a time that is viewed in your mind as a 'gift' you give yourself in which you let yourself work on yourself as it concerns your thoughts, values, memories, beliefs, and your states of mind. As you do this you'll continue to work in harmony with your 'hypnotic mind' in order to bring about the life you most desire—and be able to sustain it as you like.

WHAT IF I DON'T HAVE THE TIME

Manifesting health is no different than manifesting anything else in your life. The process I teach in this book is specifically self-hypnosis.

Now there are really, in my opinion, two cool things to know when it comes to manifesting good health. The first thing is you can work using self-hypnosis to put yourself in the right thinking state to decode what your health currently is and that you may be able to maintain it using self-hypnosis throughout your life.

I know someone who took this approach and after having done so has never been to the hospital or to see a doctor since. Now, I'm not suggesting that you don't visit your family practitioner for regular checkups, I'm just sharing what one person has done since employing self-hypnosis. This person also claims he never gets sick anymore. He mentioned to me that his seasonal allergies have since went away and haven't returned for over five years as of writing this book.

To hear this person talk about their health and well-being since employing self-hypnosis is fascinating to listen to. It's inspiration, in fact.

Another approach I find really cool is the idea that you can implement good health measures such as exercise, yoga, and other physical activities into your life that are quite hypnotic in and of themselves. What this lets you do is work on other aspects of yourself and manifesting other things you desire into your life while you maintain your health at the same time.

I have to mention that this is an approach I utilize on a daily basis. I walk my dog down to a public nature park that seldom gets visitors. There's rolling hills there and tons of privacy and nature. What I do is walk her around the nature park while at the same time contemplating ideas under hypnosis. I do this each time I walk her, several times a day, for an hour or more each time we go out. In this way I am letting my 'hypnotic mind' take control, while I briskly walk her, letting her explore and chase after squirrels and the occasional kitty cat.

I don't measure exactly how much walking I get in each day, but I know it takes up a sizeable portion of my day. In this way I get exercise without critically thinking about having to exercise. Critically thinking about exercising is one reason so many people get out of the habit of exercising, because exercising is thought, at least critically, as work and something not exactly pleasant to embark on doing.

So there are upsides to this approach. I'm doing amazing change work on myself, working on my personal and professional development, using self-hypnosis, while at the same time unconsciously getting the exercise needed to maintain a healthy lifestyle.

While you keep fit, the self-hypnosis helps you to shift negative thought-patterns, old values that don't help you get what you want out of life, as well as how health is achieve, while also your beliefs about health and why it is important to maintain it, into a positive direction that permits you to live out a happy and healthy life.

These two approaches are ones that I find powerfully uplifting when it comes to focusing on better health.

I recently heard a talk given by Dr. Deepak Chopra, who is a prominent figure in the health and wellness industry, who discussed how it is now common place for health practitioners to prescribe to patients alternative health treatments that go beyond merely traditional medical practices. Preventative health can mean the difference between experiencing good health longer and having to then spend costly amounts of money on medical care in the short term. What you do now matters more than you think and realize. My encouragement is to apply a health routine in your life that allows you to accomplish two things simultaneously; namely: (a) exercise your body in a hypnotic way, and (b) utilize this hypnotic experience to promote positive mental health as well, in order to manifest the best life for yourself. If you take this approach to health you'll have the time to accomplish more than just good physical health. I'd even argue that if you take this approach you'll be able to accomplish more in less time than you would otherwise, because you will be able to accomplish more when you're healthy than when you're not. Also, you'll be able to think hypnotically intentionally in a way that affects you positively psychologically.

CHAPTER NOTES

In this chapter we discussed health, and how regular exercise can be a powerful hypnosis in and of itself. We also explored some of the reasons why maintaining good health is so important for well-being and specifically when it comes to manifesting what you want out of life.

We also defined what good health; determining that it's not just being physically healthy, yet also mentally healthy as well. The mental affects the physical and vice-versa. When you are healthy mentally it is more likely you'll be physically fit, because the two are interconnected. Your physiology affects your mental state—for example, if you observe most depressed people, you'll find their physiology is slumped shoulders and a downward gaze. When they have changed their physiology to having an upright posture and focusing straight ahead the depression, in many instances, stops being a problem. Likewise, when people don't get enough exercise and begin living a sedentary lifestyle, often times their mental state shifts to one that's less beneficial for them in terms of manifesting what they desire out of life.

Besides this, we also looked at the process of 'how' people can remain healthy. This took us to identifying the right types of exercise programs that will be most beneficial to us, while lessening the negative connotation that the word 'exercise' conjures up in the mind of most people. How we achieve this is by finding activities that keep us regularly active, but also allow us to do change work mentally at the same time utilizing self-hypnosis as a means to affect positive changes and outcomes in our lives.

Lastly, we discussed 'time', which is the biggest excuse people make for not doing exercise. We reframed this argument to contrast how exercise can actually help us accomplish more than just staying physically fit; namely, it can help us accomplish more by giving us time to meditate on our day, what we need to get done, yet, also, it provides us an outlet to doing our mental manifesting exercises as well, which we've already learnt is so incredibly important to do in order to manifest our needs, desires, and dreams.

ACTION STEPS

The following action steps are meant to help you think about what you want, to bring about what you think. Please do the exercises even if you've done them before in the past on some other course. Your compliance is evidence of your real desire to manifest outwardly what you most seek, desire, and dream of having, experiencing, and achieving in life.

I. Take an assessment of your health. Note down in your hypnotic journal what your regular routine is, if any, that you do to promote health and wellness in your life. Write down an plan that is immediately actionable, if need be, that will allow you to exercise hypnotically so you get in your exercise time, yet also which will let you work on your own personal development and give you time to communicate to your 'hypnotic mind' so that you may continually nourish the thought-seeds you've planted there.

II. Write down your experiences and discoveries over the next seven days as you exercise hypnotically both your body and mind. Take note of any insights you have, or realizations that come to you intuitively. At the end of the seven days review these and determine if you're more or less in alignment with achieving your desired outcomes.

III. Make it a habit to assign time 'everyday' to implement this practice of hypnotic exercise. Every day, take a mental note of your experiences, and continue to journal your findings. Also, notate how much more time you seem to have now, having made time for hypnotic exercise in your life.

CHAPTER 5

BUSINESS

Whether you work for a business, or you own a business, success in business has very much to do with your mindset, your training, and your ability to problem solve. Businesses rely on individuals with a proclivity to affect changes within an organization that are positive, and through which growth happens. All of this being said an organization is in many ways like a single individual. One things a business and an individual share in common is an eventual death. Nothing or no 'thing' lasts forever; human or otherwise. In time every business will cease to exist.

This aside I want to talk about business success and the way you can stimulate your business or career in order to create both growth opportunities for your business and yourself. Many small business owners work around the clock to grow their young start-up companies, focusing on: getting the marketing right; getting the sales coming in; finding a client base; keeping customers happy; and having a good product that will stand the test of time, just to name a few. These are all important things to consider when operating and managing a business.

The thoughts running through an individual's mind as they're working for a company, or they're engaged in activities that concern their own business can be either positive or negative whereas it effects the organization. Work place politics, for example, happen in nearly every business, in which people are challenging one another and competing against their peers to vie for higher positions where they'll have more power and control over others.

If you happen to be a small business owner, as I am, it may be that you're constantly concerned about what you're unable to do. There are only so many hours in a day and so much more that is required to get done than is humanly possible for us to do.

This type of thinking: what I've just suggested to you about not having enough time to get all the many tasks done that you need to get done is something that is not uncommon to many small business owners. What I would like to suggest is your mindset has so much to do with the success of your business. Keeping thoughts like the one I mentioned regarding not having enough time to get things done, are actually what hinders a business from succeeding often times.

Businesses are run in many ways hypnotically. Procedurally and systematically seems to be the mantra for how businesses function to take inputs and turn them into outputs. Everything is an organized system in most companies. In this way, adopting this approach to operations, businesses can, in one sense, be run on autopilot. All that is required is a person or machine to do something over and over again to achieve a same result and output level. The consistency and sameness that exists in a business process can change in time, however, as it is now the routine become actually hypnotic. People have a tendency who operate in such environments to think certain thoughts; thus, certain thought patterns happen, certain outcomes come about as a result, and you might conclude that beliefs are formed as a result of these results.

We measure success in terms of values, and what is achieved, proportional to this. We also recall times when we fail, or miss the mark. In my opinion, 'failure' should be eradicated from your vocabulary; instead, substitute 'feedback' in place of 'failure'. Feedback gives us back value, instead of taking away our resources which we view as loss.

I think it is important to realize this because your mindset and what we're conditioned to believe regarding what is a good decision versus a bad decision, what's helpful versus what's hurtful, these are mental constructs which we buy into, which for this, we must hold ourselves accountable for in our positions, and while running our companies. As a result of this I feel it is important to address such an issue in the same way I would encourage you to manifest anything; namely, by the Law of Hypnosis.

What I would have you do is be consciously aware of where your business is at the present moment, and certainly to use your logical, rational, critical thinking brain while you're in a beta state to decipher problems and to look at logical options for solving these problems. Beyond this, however, I would also have you work on your business using the Law of Hypnosis, where you will tap into your 'hypnotic mind', and in the same way you'd manifest anything, manifest your business outcomes successfully in the same manner. Doing so will bring with it hypnotic insights that otherwise wouldn't thinking logically alone.

You'd be surprised how many times, and how often someone finds an insight or solution that helps their business beyond anything their critical 'mind' could have ever come up with on its own.

This happens to me all the time whereas my business is concerned. One exercise I personally do is utilize a drowsy hypnotic state and lie down on the floor of my home-office, with a pillow behind my head, and shut my eyes and let my 'hypnotic mind' go to and find a solution for whatever problem I may be facing. Most of the decisions I make in my business are done while under the influence of hypnosis.

WHY IS HYPNOSIS IMPORTANT TO USE IN YOUR BUSINESS

I've mentioned how businesses are comprised of various systems and parts working together to produce specific outcomes that result in sustainability and growth for that business. These systems work on autopilot to produce the types of consistent results business owners and managers require. When change does happen, it usually happens slowly, by adopting a conservative approach to change management.

Business owners can become fearful a major abruption could immediately alter the consistency of the results they're currently sustaining, and not for the good. The idea for most business owners is to implement small changes in order to test if a change will create a positive effect on a business. In this way, if an initiative is implemented, and shown to be successful, it can then be adopted over multiple departments, or channels, or other areas in which a business operates out of. Small changes in this way can be scaled larger when the changes are tested and proved to be successful in small markets.

Marketing departments often will release a new product to a sample of their target market to determine the efficacy of their marketing messages. If the marketing is not effective, they can scrap the marketing messages or product, and refocus onto new ideas. If it is shown to be effective the marketing department can scaled over the rest of the target market.

You see, now, that companies are willing to accept and embrace change, but tend to do so in small measures, which are less costly and thus less risky for an organization.

Many people I've personally known who embrace the Law of Hypnosis begin by testing manifesting skills by first manifesting something that is more believable. Testing the waters in this way helps them more believe in the Law of Hypnosis. Once found to be true it is easier for them to scale to much more desired things they wish to manifest.

In business utilizing your 'hypnotic mind' can give you a real advantage over those who don't. You see, the reason for this has to do with the insights and inspirations that you'll receive as a result of utilizing your 'hypnotic mind'. When you tap into the 'hypnotic mind' using self-hypnosis as the means you start to magnetize solutions into your life and the life of your business that help it grow prodigiously.

One of the issues I dealt with when first becoming a writer was the competition, as I saw it then, regarding great books already written on the same topics I wanted to write about. This was somewhat discouraging at first for me. I could read a book and wish to myself I had written it. I wanted a magic wand to wave that would allow me to get brilliant insights and original ideas to share as value to the rest of the world who were interested in my field of expertise.

What I began doing was employing the Law of Hypnosis in my life by committing to doing regular self-hypnosis. Before long I had a desk drawer packed with tons of ideas for books I wanted to write eventually. I also had ideas that were truly original which came to be as insights from my 'hypnotic mind'.

This resulted in me writing and sharing content in books other people found not only useful but as the number one contributing factor for their success in sales, marketing, and interpersonal communications. This was feedback for me that let me know insightfully that I was on the right path. I have, to date, received countless emails, comments, and even video testimonials from people telling me I've changed their lives. It is an amazing feeling, yet I'm not egotistical about it. My true objective is to provide as much value to my readers as I can, holding nothing significant back.

Now you see why it is important to utilize your 'hypnotic mind' to bring about in manifested form the results that you're truly seeking. It is also useful for ensuring a clean and clear mindset, which is beneficial in business.

WHAT CAN THE LAW OF HYPNOSIS DO FOR YOUR BUSINESS

I've already given some example of how I've personally used the law of hypnosis to help grow my own business. What I'd like to do now is give you, from my own perspective, some of the things I believe would benefit most people should they decide to employ the law of hypnosis into their own business.

First and foremost, businesses are typically run logically. Most of the people coming out of MBA programs are taught critical thinking skills in order to solve complex business problems. These are things done through structural and mathematical computations where reasoning is employed for measuring the efficacy of an implement compared to other implements that could be chosen instead. These types of skills carry over into implementing process improvement plans, and other types of management frameworks.

Sometime ago, some years back, there was a phenomenon that seemed to take place as I recall, where many businesses were foregoing the hiring of MBAs and people who were coming out of business colleges, opting instead to hire for these positions those with fine arts and liberal arts degrees. These people were employed because there was perceived a need for more creative types to inject creative insights into existing business practices. Even some CEOs were chosen from backgrounds in a liberal arts education.

One thing hypnosis lets you do is think outside the box or logic. This happens because the 'hypnotic mind' doesn't work logically in the same way the critical thinking 'mind' happens to operate. It works in pictures, images, and insights; it takes everything in from the senses that the critical 'mind' is unable to pick-up on and perceive. It stores this information inside the 'hypnotic mind' to be accessed whenever needed. What you can do is tap into this 'hypnotic mind' to uncover brilliant solutions that would not be taught in business schools.

This can give you a real edge, because it's not predictable. The types of insights I'm talking about you receiving are insights that are truly unique; that is, they're so unique that some people will think you're brilliant when you implement them. These can very much help your business succeed and grow where others won't, because nobody will have been taught these insights in any old business school.

Your critical 'mind' is limited in its ability to perceive things imaginatively. It operates in black and white, right and wrong, good and bad, a good decision or a bad decision, a logical decision or an irrational decision, and it looks at the world in terms of these types of linear models, which have been scaled down from something much larger so that they can be understood much easier and quicker. Most of models are constructed in this exact fashioning. In business schools, like Harvard, and others, case studies are dissected in order to model solution, which have worked for other companies in order to adopt them into a blueprint that can be readily copied by other business leaders, for the purpose of achieving the same high-quality results.

Again this gets us back to the idea and thinking that what's worked in the past will work in the future. The problem, however, with this type of thinking and structuring can be that other businesses alongside yours are using the same models and techniques to monetize their business processes.

The benefit of utilizing a 'hypnotic' approach is that it is an approach that will bring with it great new insights which have never been before adopted. The primary benefit to adopting this approach lies in the value other business are not adopting the same insights into their business, because they simply do not have those insights. Instead they're utilizing approaches that have already been tested and put in to easily replicated models everybody else is using.

Imagine being able to implement an approach no other business has ever thought to employ. Imagine the possibilities and gains that would likely be acquired. This can give you competitive advantage.

When you look a lot of the top online internet marketers in the e-commerce industry you'll find that they have gotten to where they are in terms of abundant successfulness and earning their celebrity-like status in the world of copywriting and marketing, because of their willingness to step outside the box of traditional business and marketing practices. Instead, they've custom created new models from the insights they've received from utilizing this 'hypnotic' approach, and adopted their insights to much success.

What they do then is sell their ideas and models to other companies for a profit, while then going out to discover new ways of achieving results besides the ones they've not sold and put into the public domain.

Many of these personalities have gained their success through utilizing the power of their 'hypnotic mind' to come up with and create some of these amazing marketing ploys. I'm suggesting you do the same for your own business needs.

HOW CAN YOUR EMPLOY HYPNOSIS TO GAIN COMPETITIVE ADVANTAGE IN BUSINESS

As I've mentioned to you in the chapter titled: 'Hypnosis' the process for hypnotizing yourself and others is quite simple and a natural process that happens to us regardless of whether we're aware of it or not. It is a state where you can be aware of everything, and, yet, not aware of the very activity you're presently working on. You are working on autopilot mode doing something, while you're hypnotized and focused elsewhere. Your hypnotic mind takes you to places you currently are not physically located. Think about how amazing this experience is, and consider that you're transcending with your 'hypnotic mind' both space and time. I find it utterly captivating to think about, personally.

In this way you are coming up with insights, thoughts, fantasies, stories, and methods for achieving success in your businesses and personal life. The techniques for self-hypnosis are easy, in my opinion. You simply pick a point on the wall in a room where you won't be disturbed for a period of time, and concentrate all your focus and energy there. In a quick period, you'll begin to notice your breathing start to slow down and deepen, your gaze will soften, you'll start to find your thoughts quietening and you'll begin to enter a hypnotic trance states. Putting yourself under hypnosis is as simple as this. You know what this feels like, because you experience it every day, only most of the time unconsciously.

While you're hypnotizing yourself, be consciously aware that you're hypnotizing yourself so that you can be lucid while hypnotized. This will let you impress suggestions into your 'hypnotic mind'. This will let you also direct and focus your thinking patterns in a way that is helpful for manifesting your needs, wants, and dreams.

You'll find that as you apply this self-hypnosis technique that you'll start to become more insightful about things you didn't know before consciously. These insights should be noted down immediately after your hypnosis experience so you can remember them and study them to determine how you might usefully apply them to your business.

What's more you can also suggest to yourself, while hypnotized, that certain business outcomes will transpire—for example, your business will grow fast and wide and bring with this expansion more value for society to benefit from in a positive way.

> *"If you can dream it, then you can achieve it. You will get all you want in life if you help enough other people get what they want."*
>
> —Zig Ziglar

WHAT IF UTILIZING THE LAW OF HYPNOSIS DOES NOT SEEM TO WORK FOR YOUR BUSINESS

One thing the Law of Hypnosis helps you achieve is clarity and insight. These insights can be employed in your business if you choose implement them. This is entirely your choice, and would tell you from experience that not every insight or idea I've had is one that I have installed into the inner-workings of my business.

Thoughts can be positive or negative. Much of this depends on your mindset. It will depend on how much effort and attention you've given to the exercises throughout this book, which are there to help you achieve the value, as well as determine exactly what it is you desire most for your life—and get it!

Once you work on yourself and you are able to objectively look at your old thought patterns, beliefs, values, memories, and old ways of feeling and being in terms of your states of mind, and you determine how useless these things are for you today, and that new behaviors, a different mindset, emphasis on new values is determined, more useful beliefs are discovered, and you become discriminate in your states and how you feel and how much more useful this new way of perceiving is for you, you'll start to see incredible results happening almost instantly by the results produced for you by your 'hypnotic mind'. You can really start to get excited because this feat is truly astonishing to experience and see unfold. You learn insightfully that you have the power to change your life and the life of your business.

Now you see instant change is possible through taking a few simple steps to change the way your perceive various aspects of yourself to be, while using the Law of Hypnosis in your favor to help you bring about what you think about from the 'chitta' or 'invisible stuff' that your 'hypnotic mind' uses to create externally, for you, in order for you to be able to experience thoughts with your five senses as 'real'.

If you do not see results right away it means you may want to take a look at your perceptions about what's possible for yourself and your business. You may find that you have old beliefs hiding from plain sight that have you believing that in order to be successful in business you have to be 'cut-throat' in your business practices, or work 100 hours a week, or that you must sacrifice away the first five years before you can realize a profit, and so on. Some of these ideas may sound familiar, wouldn't you say? You must identify these types of old beliefs which are holding you back, because of your buying-into-them as being the 'truth'. Remember, a belief is something you believe, whether it is true or not.

The same must be done whereas 'values', 'thought-patterns', 'bad past experiences', and 'poor states of mind' are concerned; that is to say, if you want to impregnate your desires and dreams in the fertile fields of your 'hypnotic mind'. Once you clarify what you want and pursue it using the 'Law of Hypnosis' nothing can stand in the way of your successes.

CHAPTER NOTES

In this chapter we looked at business, comparing it in many ways to a single individual. This was done intentionally to make a business more relatable to you in terms of understanding yourself. Businesses are complex entities, but so are human beings. We have needs and want, yet so also do businesses. There are many parallels between the human and the business. Businesses were modeled after the human being in terms of the processes for producing. Businesses have objectives and goals, while also human beings have objective and goals. Both businesses and human beings will eventually fall from their rise and not withstand death. It happens for everyone and every business.

We also looked some of the reasons why hypnosis is important for you to use to profit your business. I taught you that you can businesses in and of themselves are very much a hypnotic function, because in them exists many revolving processes. These processes are what keep a business consistently performing and producing the outputs and results business owners and managers expect.

Next we discovered some of the ways the Law of Hypnosis could be used to help a business succeed, where others might fail. For instance, we discovered the 'creative' and 'emotional' effects that could be achieved from using the 'hypnotic mind' to bring a business more to life and create new opportunities for growth by 'idea generation'.

Thereafter, we focused our attention on how businesses could exploit the Law of Hypnosis to gain 'competitive advantage' by harnessing this law to bring about unique business strategies that aren't taught in business schools, in order to differentiate our businesses from all the other competition out there using the same models as everyone else uses. This differentiation gives us something that is not identifiable by our competition, and it can easily come by way of the insights we receive using our 'hypnotic mind' and the 'Law of Hypnosis' to receive such bursts of insights while in a 'THETA' state (i.e., deep hypnotic state).

ACTION STEPS

The following action steps are meant to help you think about what you want, to bring about what you think. Please do the exercises even if you've done them before in the past on some other course. Your compliance is evidence of your real desire to manifest outwardly what you most seek, desire, and dream of having, experiencing, and achieving in life.

I. Introspect in how many and what ways your business or career is hypnotic, and how you might exploit the hypnotic aspect of your position in this business to prosper yourself and the company. Write down these insights in your hypnotic journal.

II. Use self-hypnosis to impress your business desires and dreams onto the wall of your 'hypnotic mind'. If you feel hesitation, or intuit any problems doing this, stop, and introspect any hidden beliefs about business that could be standing in your way of business success. There are many ideas people form about organizations, capitalism, what's fair in business and what's not, that it is not uncommon for individuals working in an organization or building their own company to have a few hang-ups which prevent them from trouncing defeat. Once you discover these beliefs that are likely holding you back declare to your 'hypnotic mind' that you no longer believe these false and misleading beliefs anymore.

III. Play a mental movie in your mind that shows you your business the way you would like to see it as an afterthought to what you desire for it to be in the near future. Feel how you'll feel. See what you'll see. Hear what you'll hear. Make the experience as real as possible. Then believe that it is happening now to come about through the power of your 'hypnotic mind'.

CHAPTER 6

WEALTH

Wealth is an illusory term in my opinion. I say this because what one person considers wealth another considers something vastly different. It depends on an individual's perspective to know what one things wealth is defined as.

Achieving wealth in your life where money is concerned can be a challenge for many people. Everybody has a different identification with money; to some it means survival, to others it means power, yet, still, to some the definition is as broad as these two poles. The questions you may have to ask are: "What are my financial goals?" "What would I like to have?" "What do I need to live out the life I want to live?"

When people think about money sometimes they get a little excited or anxious. The thought of being able to make an extra hundred dollars on a bi-monthly paycheck or an extra thousand-dollars on a single sale made, or an extra million on a single transaction, in a single day, may be enough to get an individual excited.

What's in one person's reality may however be light years away from another. What one person perceives as a lot of money, to another may be nothing significant whatsoever.

Money is a form of exchange. It is where we trade paper bills for something of value that is represented in terms of the amount of those paper bills we receive.

For many people, running a business, developing a product, which will help and be of value to members of society in some capacity, money may be thought of as a byproduct of providing such value. Instead of thinking "How much money can I amass from others," what most should be asking is "How much value can I provide to others".

> "Making money isn't hard in itself…
>
> What's hard is to earn it doing something worth devoting one's life to."
>
> —Carlos Ruiz Zafón, *The Shadow of the Wind*

When you provide value you take on an equal return back in the form of money. One thing people get caught up in is judging people who work menial jobs. We question why on earth would someone in their 30s want to work at a fast-food restaurant, making minimum wage? We question why companies should pay minimum wage and not more for the service someone provides? We question, possibly, why a lawyer makes more than a fast-food worker? Maybe not!

It all comes down to the value that someone provides. The more value you provide the more you deserve to make monetarily. A lawyer can keep me out of prison for a lifetime, therefore I don't mind paying a lawyer more than I tip my server. It comes down to value and what you value. Again, value is what is important to you. The more important something is to you the more value it has and the more expensive you perceive it to be. When we receive more value than we pay for we may think we've gotten a 'good deal' or found 'luck' or even that the quality must 'be less' elsewise why would I pay so little. Value is relative to what each individual is conditioned to believe and think about what something's worth should be.

My father was born in 1931, he grew up at a time when a bowl of soup could be bought for a nickel in a dine-in restaurant. To pay this little, nowadays, is unthinkable for us to imagine. Our perceptions have changed; we now believe a bowl of soup costs upwards of a few dollars, maybe more than one-hundred nickels it would cost us today for a bowl of the same kind of soup.

My point for telling you this is to contrast the difference in value from yesteryear to today. Things change and no-thing stays the same, as mentioned earlier. Likewise values change, beliefs change, memories change, people's states of mind change, and also do peoples' thought-patterns. All of these change and evolve. I mention this that you might release some of the grip on your firmly attached beliefs, values, thoughts, memories, and state of mind. It is okay to embrace change and not be afraid if it. Change will get you what you want so long as you apply the Law of Hypnosis.

In this chapter I want to share with you about wealth and how you can achieve more of it; specifically, for getting what you want by having enough money to purchase it. Now, the suggestion I just made, regarding value exchanged for money, is again, another presupposition. It is a belief and nothing more, which has been conceptualized and shared throughout history one generation to the next. It comes about through the values carried down and handed off to others another generation down and so on; namely, through value statements like what my father always advocated to me: "If I didn't earn it, I don't want it." This was him saying he didn't want something for nothing. He didn't ever accept any handouts that I can remember, but, rather preferred to be responsible and held accountable for his own results. He didn't believe in accepting something without giving something back in exchange. His pride kept him from receiving kindness from others. Many people share this type of thinking. It transitions over to being a belief, and the belief becomes a value representing what is important to an individual. We make decisions based on the values, the thoughts, the beliefs, the memories or past accounts that have taken place, and the states of mind we're in at the time a decision is to be made. Making the wrong decisions can keep us in poverty, lacking and limited in resources, and keep us bound up like a prisoner in our own mind. We can surely suffer for it too.

To free yourself, I suggest you begin utilizing the power of your 'hypnotic mind' embracing the Law of Hypnosis openly, suspending your doubts, and being grateful for this newfound knowledge which opens up the floodgates of prosperity for you to be able to receive as much wealth as you require to be able to do all the things in life you wish to be able to do without worry or fear of never having enough to go around. You always have enough to go around, and money is a vehicle to take you to the places and experiences in life you wish to navigate and give you the things you desire and dream of owning.

There still, for some, exists this opportunity that doesn't seem to exists for the majority of people in the world. You see three or four percent of the world's wealth is shared by 96 or 97 per cent of the world's population. The vast majority of wealth; that is, the 97 to 98% of all money in existence is owned by only three or four percent of the world's population. How is it that so few own so much and so many own so little by comparison? It's a conundrum that may be solvable only were people not so easily influenced by other people; yet, still were able to control their own 'hypnotic mind' utilizing the 'Law of Hypnosis'.

As I've insinuated subtly by gently inferring that some people have so much money, while the vast majority have so little, this seems to be a phenomenon that happens one generation to the next. There are the 'haves' and the 'have-nots'. Sometimes someone in poverty, raised to be poor, will achieve a great amount of financial success and raise themselves out of poverty and into the top 1% of income earners. Most look at this as a great accomplishment. Other may wonder how it is possible.

The answer lies in one's ability to communicate with their 'hypnotic mind' and suggest to the 'hypnotic mind' what is wished for and believe that the Law of Hypnosis will manifest it back out to them in the form of an external result, i.e. 'reality'. If you can simply do this you will help your finances is so many ways, you won't realize how incredibly easy it was for you to go from owing money to being owed money. It really is that easy; yet, you must 'ask' in order to 'receive'.

Think about all I've shared with you about money so far. I've listed in many ways 'beliefs' and 'limitations' that many people are conditioned to believe. I've talked about the values people have regarding the value of money. I've shared with you why most people remain poor or middle class, while only a small few ever get rich. People have all sorts of ideas that limit the way that they might receive income also: believing that it takes starting a business, winning some lottery, inheriting a fortune, investing in the stock market, buying up real estate to hold on to. These seem like plausible answers for getting rich; however, in their own right, they also represent limitations, because there are literally infinite ways in which a person may attain wealth. These are only a few possibilities, but they too could be ways of losing money. Think about it.

Utilizing the law of hypnosis requires one fundamental thing: do nothing except let your hypnotic mind the Law of Hypnosis to bring into your life what you desire. You still need to align your thought patterns, beliefs, values, past memories, and current state of mind congruently with your 'hypnotic mind' and specifically what it is you want so you know you will receive it to the point that you believe you've already received it.

One thing many people who pray find is when they believe without a shadow of a doubt that their prayers will be answered they usually are. When they recognize the power of prayer, they continue praying for the things they desire most until they receive them. Prayer is a form of hypnosis, in which we put on hold our critical thinking that tells us what's possible and what's not, and suspend our doubts to allow for something to happen irrespective of logic and reason. The last resort prayer to a supernatural being believing that miracles do happen—leads one to realize God or some supernatural power is looking over you.

I'm here to tell you that miracles don't have to be miracles, and you can have what you want, without question, without logic, without reason, and all you have to do to achieve wealth in your life is to do self-hypnosis and implant hypnotic suggestions into your 'hypnotic mind' and receive your result with expectancy. It will happen. It doesn't matter how good you are; how bad you've been; who you know; what you were brought up to believe; or where you live—the Law of Hypnosis works for everybody regardless of any of these things. You just have to believe and then you'll receive—guaranteed! It's that simple!

WHY HAVE I NOT ACHIEVED FINANCIAL SUCCESS AND SUSTAINED IT

The reason you've not achieved financial success yet, nor sustain it if you've ever in the past achieved a measure of financial prosperity, or what you believed financial success was, is because of your erratic mind. When you had money, and this is assuming you've ever a good deal of it save at some point in your life, the way people treated you was different, wasn't it? Your friends didn't regard you as they might have when you had barely two dimes two rub together on a good day.

There are challenges that come with having money. Perhaps you were taken for granted by someone you knew who made the assumption you could afford to pay for everybody's meal when a group of you and your friends met up for dinner. Maybe it was expected of you to buy them something expensive for them, since you had more money than them. Maybe you had people beating down a path to your doorway begging money off of you. I could have been anything remotely similar to any one of these scenarios I've brought forth here.

Some people get name called who have money. Some get excluded from social groups. Some find it difficult to relate to their old friends who are still broke and struggling. Some find it hard not to spend their money and to foolishly give it away to people who will have it spent by weeks end. There are a lot of things that happen as a result of having money, aren't there?

When people experience the uneasiness that comes with having an abundance of money they've never had before, and with scenarios like I've mentioned, they have a tendency to quickly get rid of the problem, i.e. the money. They spend it foolishly, quickly, and find themselves broke well before any prudent person would.

I can earnestly relate to this type of situation. Once upon a time I had, what I considered, a lot of money. I skimped, horded, saved, went without, and over a period of about three years had more interest being earned off of the money I had saved in the stock market than I was earning in a single year working a mid-level management job. I was feeling pretty good about what I had achieved. But, this feeling quickly went away.

When I made the mistake of sharing my good-fortune and started even to give advice to friends I quickly found myself without any. I was called a cheap scape, a miser, a scrooge, and a litany of other foul labels. It honestly hurt my feelings. These were people I deeply cared about, and now they were arguing with me that I should pick up the entire bill anytime we met up for lunch or some extracurricular activity. When I refused, they refused to be my friend. Who needs friends like that, right?

When I became an outcast from my peer group I blamed money for it. I started to devalue money and see it not as a blessing but as a curse. My beliefs about money changed. It was now an evil and not a piece of good fortune. As you might have guessed by now, reading this account, I manifested something into my life that would get rid of the problem, and make me poor again.

In a single day, I lost nearly every dollar I had invested in the stock market. It was gone in a day, what had taken me three years of being overly conservative and robbing myself of all the blessings money can buy.

Needless to say I fell into a deep depression. A depression so deep it nearly did me in. I'm resilient though, and so I bounced back and better than ever in a way that completely took me by surprise, and in a way that didn't leave me doing without just to be able to get ahead. I was able to achieve much more success than ever before while also being able to do only what made me happy, all by using the Law of Hypnosis to manifest my needs, desires, and dreams.

If you've never had money, then chances are you're ready to start living a more abundant life now and a life that you can be thrilled to wake up every morning to embrace fully; without fear or worry or anxiety about how you'll be able to afford what it is you want and need.

This is why it is important to take hold of these principles and the Law of Hypnosis now so that you can start having what it is you desire most out of life.

The reason you've never achieved financial abundance and wealth up to this point or been able to sustain it has to do with, again, your values, beliefs, thought-patterns, past affiliations, and your state of mind. I'm here to tell you that when you get these five things in check and aligned in a way that you can be all on board with receiving from your 'hypnotic mind' everything you desire—it will happen without question.

I want you to understand that you've not failed to become wealthy, you've simply not been taught 'how' to take advantage of the Law of Hypnosis to manifest into your life what it is you want, i.e. to become wealthy.

WHAT DO I NEED TO KNOW BEFORE I LEARN HOW TO BECOME WEALTHY BY HARNESSING THE LAW OF HYPNOSIS

What you need to know before I teach you how to become wealthy by harnessing the Law of Hypnosis is are a few key points. First you need to have a reason 'why' you want to be wealthy, that you can associate wealth with, and this needs to be a logical reason and something you can wrap your mind around and justify commonsensically.

Typically when people are setting goals they will create a 'why' statement, and this 'why' statement is put in place to help keep them motivated and fixated on what it is they want. A big requirement you need to keep in mind regardless of what you're deliberately attracting into your life, using the Law of Hypnosis is the principle what you think about you bring about.

Focusing on your 'why' will keep you logically focused toward the direction of what it is you want and *not* what you don't want.

The second thing you need to be aware of when manifesting wealth into your life is the old beliefs about money you may be clinging onto. For this reason, you need to evaluate yourself inquiring about old beliefs about how you value money, how you opinion money, and then you need to make changes where necessary. You can't in one breath be telling yourself you want to have money and achieve a wealthy abundant life, and then in another breath tell yourself that money is the root of all evil, because you'll be uprooting those plants that are growing healthy and strong in your 'hypnotic mind' destroying any possibility that this crop will produce for you the tangible financial results you're desiring.

So real, real, important: You must identify any and all preconceived notions you have about money and eradicate those immediately—they serve no positive good—they're weeds that will destroy the financial crops you've planted and tended to that are already growing in your 'hypnotic mind'.

The third point you need to understand in order to be able to manifest 'anything' including 'wealth' is that you must have faith in the Law of Hypnosis and the 'hypnotic mind'. You don't have to have a personal relationship with your 'hypnotic mind', and in fact, I find it better to regard it as some great mystery, and I don't try understanding it beyond that. To try an understand the 'hypnotic mind' would require a conscious critical and mindful examination of it, and because of the nature of the 'hypnotic mind' and it being the 'emotional mind' or the mind that doesn't operate through logic and reason, I don't see logically how it's possible, or realistic, that one could understand it beyond the 'hypnotic mind' model I present to you if only for serving as a 'map' but not the actual 'territory' itself. Let's leave it a mystery; yet, have faith that it works as beautifully as a child's vivid imagination works to inspire, entertain, and bring about whatever your heart desires.

HOW TO BECOME WEALTHY USING THE LAW OF HYPNOSIS

Once you've addressed any issues that you have with money as it pertains to your values, beliefs, memories concerning money from your past, your frequent thought-patterns concerning all things money related that tend to be habitual thoughts floating around, and your state of mind is ready to start using the Law of Hypnosis to ascertain what it is you want to accomplish whereas wealth is concerned, the next step is much easier.

The first thing you must do is regularly take advantage your 'alpha' states or else regularly use self-hypnosis daily to begin the process of communicating with your 'hypnotic mind'. A lot of people get lost when it comes to having a conversation with your 'hypnotic mind' because they're really not sure how to give a suggestion to it. I think the reason has to do with the logical reasoning that when we give a command or order or 'suggestion' to someone we must be careful how we come across to that person. If we're not careful the individual may reject what we tell them outright. This is true of the 'hypnotic mind' as well, though you should by now have methodically worked through your hang-ups about money, and therefore are in a prime position to be discussing money with your 'hypnotic mind' without the 'critical faculty' outright rejecting your suggestions. The suggestions you implant to your 'hypnotic mind' should be consistent with what your logical mind wants. This goes a long way in having your 'critical faculty' accepting your suggestions, because already your critical 'mind' has accepted them, so it goes without reason that your suggestions are logical.

This so, you want to feel in alignment with what you want to ask of your 'hypnotic mind' and when all is said and done you want to walk away from the hypnotic interaction feeling as though all parts of you are on board with what you want. If you don't, then you'll want to revisit the 'hypnotic mind' in while again under 'hypnosis' and reassert what it is you want. You must 'believe' you'll receive what you are asking for once your interaction is over. You must 'value' what it is you want and expect to get. You must reflect on times in your life when what you wanted would have assisted you in great measure making your life much better. You must keep both your conscious and unconscious thoughts aligned with what you want and not start to think incongruently. You must be sure to keep your state of mind congruent with how you'll feel once you receive what you desire, i.e. wealth.

To achieve the hypnotic state let me reiterate the process again: (a) focus your attention on some object or spot on your wall in a room you will not be disturbed for at least 30 minutes, (b) bypass your critical faculty by having your values, beliefs, thought-patterns, past experiences, and your current state of mind all in alignment with what it is you want to manifest, i.e. wealth, (c) stimulate your hypnotic mind by letting yourself enter a deep hypnotic trance, (d) remain just lucid enough to feed your suggestions to your 'hypnotic mind'. Then once you deliver your hypnotic commands let yourself come back up out of hypnosis and rejoin your consciousness. This exercise is easy to implement and follow and one that you can use over and over and over again to manifest what you want into your life, time and time again.

The next phase of this process is simply maintaining the expectation and 'knowing' that you'll receive 'wealth' as soon as your 'hypnotic mind' takes your thoughts and creates your future in the context of a future space and time. In this way, 'matter' or what you want, will exist in the space-time continuum.

What you can do is keep a watch out for things to start happening to bring about 'wealth' into your life. This could be, for instance, if you happen to be in 'sales' selling a new major account who will be a likely long term customer for years to come. It could be if you're working in fast-food that you lose your job, or that you come into contact with just the right person to help you start another line of work. There are literally so many possibilities and possibilities you won't even consciously be able to come up with on your own, I've found it best not to think about 'how' things will enter your life, but rather to simply 'expect' them without wondering 'why'. The minute you start assuming 'how' is the minute you start placing limitation or feeding different suggestions to your 'hypnotic mind'—don't do this, because you want to stay completely aligned with what you want, giving your hypnotic mind free reign to bring it about however it sees fit. Trust it, remember!

WHAT IF I DON'T ATTRACT WEALTH IMMEDIATELY, THEN WHAT

I would like to tell you to quit worrying so much, but I've been exactly where you are right now. Waiting is something nobody wants to do. We think inverse to this; believing that we must 'act' in order to get anything done. This is a dilemma for all new time 'manifestors' because it takes them time to relax and become laid back about the process. Trust that your 'hypnotic mind' is doing its best to bring things into your reality in the 'best' way possible.

This being said, there are times when you wait, and wait, and it seems like nothing ever happens. I've found that when this is the case, it's different than just waiting on your 'hypnotic mind' to work its mysterious magic. It's more usually a case of your verbiage, that hasn't been corrected.

One thing, very important, you need to understand about your 'hypnotic mind' is that it is 'not' logical or able to reason meaning in the same way your critical 'mind' is able to do. Remember in the beginning when we talked about 'hypnosis' and I mentioned to you that the conscious 'mind' (i.e., your cortex) is responsible for 'language'. It is! It's also easy to forget this!

A lot of times people use 'negatives' which are inferred in language to mean something 'other than' what is being suggested—for example, the statement: "I'm not going to the movies!" This is implying you'll be anywhere 'other than' the movies. This is 'logical'. Your 'hypnotic mind' doesn't see where you'll not be, it only sees the picture of the 'movies' and therefore assumes you'll be going to the movies. So you end up by some mysterious means finding yourself coming into an awareness with a 'movie theatre' whether by a poster image, passing by one, someone talking about one they've been to, etc. All this passes by your conscious 'mind' and goes undetected and you assume it to be 'coincidental' in terms of its occurrence in your reality. Guess what!...It's not!

I tell you this because when you say or think such things as: "I don't want to be poor!" or "I'm not manifesting being broke anymore!" your 'hypnotic mind' reads these as suggestions only not in the way you want it too. It reads them in the positive, because it doesn't understand 'language' only pictures; namely: "I want to be poor!" and "I'm manifesting being broke!" You have to, for this reason, as I keep reiterating throughout this book, ONLY THINK ABOUT POSITIVE THINGS YOU WANT AND TALK ABOUT POSITIVE THINGS YOU WANT! NEVER EVER, EVER, EVER, USE THE WORDS: **Don't, Not,** and **No!** I learned this actually from another book written by Michael Losier, which I make reference of in the bibliography at the back of this book.

If you are finding that it is taking you an incredibly long time to manifest 'wealth' into your life, take an objective look at your language and how you've been using it verbally as well as when engaged in 'self-talk'. It could very well be the problem hanging you up from growing those money trees in your 'hypnotic mind'.

CHAPTER NOTES

In this chapter we looked at how to manifest wealth and abundance into your life using the Law of Hypnosis to accomplish this. We began with an extensive examination of how people think about wealth, what happens when a person experiences wealth, and how wealth affects different people differently.

Next we looked at why people don't achieve financial success or if they do come into wealth why they're unable to sustain it lastingly. Most of the time wealth isn't created due to the nature of the erratic mind constantly contradicting what it wants. People have a difficult time throughout their life determining what's important to them and an even harder time making decisions. Let's face it, for many people the thought of making a decision to move their life in a particular direction is off-putting and causes anxiety, worry, and panic to set in. It's easier for many people to simply ignore making crucial decision that will get them what they want out of life.

One reason, we've determined for this, is that often times when people do get what they want other's, i.e. their peers and family, become jealous and tend to force the person who's actually made a success of it away from them. Remember, and this is important: Like attracts like. Unsuccessful people have difficult time remaining in the same space of successful people; successful people, likewise have a difficult time occupying the same space as unsuccessful people. Be prepared for this to happen when you do become fabulously wealthy. It really has nothing to do with who your true friends are; that is to say, it has everything to do with like attracting like. Do not judge people who can't associate with you anymore. Wish future success for them and let them live out their life apart from their jealousy concerning what you have.

We also explored, related to this, how misaligned values, beliefs, pasts, thought patterns, and states of mind, play a vital role in what you manifest and what you don't. In order to maneuver into the 'how' you must first shore up any issues you have that would likely prevent you from manifesting wealth into your life.

The next thing we went over was the importance of creating a 'why' statement. This, we determined, was to both motivate you but also keep you focused on wealth and achieving it. In this section we also discussed the importance of having faith in the Law of Hypnosis, even though we said that it wasn't necessary to know much about the mystery of the 'hypnotic mind' only to understand the general process through which we are able to manifest wealth into our physical reality.

Then we flipped over to the 'how' to learn in what way would become financially prosperous and achieve abundant wealth into our life. Primarily this involves taking advantage of naturally occurring 'alpha' states to utilize these hypnotic states to implant our desires and suggestions into the 'hypnotic mind' so that they would be planted on the good ground where prosperity lies dormant, waiting to sprout into our lives. We said 'self-hypnosis' is an alternative method for achieving an alpha and theta state for the purpose of planting these seeds of suggestion. One other thing we covered was the importance of remaining lucid while under hypnosis in order to intentionally plant the desire seeds semi-consciously while under hypnosis. This is the equivalent of when people lucidly dream at night, knowing that they are dreaming, yet dreaming none the less. This gives you a measure of control that is beneficial for really being in full alignment with your desires.

The last area we covered was to look at what if you don't see immediate results, then what? I told you not to worry first of all, because worry only leads you down the path to getting what you don't want. I also shared the linguistic lesson on why it is important never to say: don't, not, and no. This includes, of course any negative contraction, especially 'can't'. Part of the reason for this is that language is logical and not picked up by your 'hypnotic mind' the same way it is interpreted logically by your 'mind'. The other part has to do with emotional anchors associated with words. Words have feelings associated to them and these feeling can act incongruently to erase the positive work that you've already begun as it concerns manifesting your needs desires and dreams. *You don't want to thwart you efforts!* See, that last sentence is an example of what I mean, instead I should have said to you: Keep positively aligned with your good efforts and keep manifesting wealth and abundance into your life. Be careful how you word things and what you say. It will not only help you to become a master hypnotic manifestor, but it will also help you to become an excellent communicator. The better you can communicate what you want to your 'hypnotic mind' the better manifestor you'll be becoming.

ACTION STEPS

The following action steps are meant to help you think about what you want, to bring about what you think. Please do the exercises even if you've done them before in the past on some other course. Your compliance is evidence of your real desire to manifest outwardly what you most seek, desire, and dream of having, experiencing, and achieving in life.

I. Identify all the preconceived notions you have concerning money and write them in your hypnotic journal. Using self-hypnosis plant the hypnotic suggestion necessary to rid your 'mind' and 'hypnotic mind' of these negative hindrances.

II. Hypnotize yourself and tell your hypnotic mind that you want to be wealthy and that you plant the seeds of wealth in your 'hypnotic mind' so that this will result in your outer external world. Keep an eye out for things to start changing in your life, and know that this is your 'hypnotic mind' creating the environment for you to be wealthy and sustain being wealthy.

III. Make yourself intentionally observant of all your language patterns, as these reflect your thought patterns, and carry emotional overtones that are read by your 'hypnotic mind'. Remember that you hypnotic mind is an 'emotional' mind. If you find yourself being negative (e.g., saying, Don't, Not, or No) reframe your language to focus on the positive intent instead. Make this a habit!

CHAPTER 7

RELATIONSHIPS

I have to be upfront and tell you I'm not a relationship expert, per se. I've been in a long term relationship with someone for many years. She and I share a very healthy relationship. We have a lot of respect for one another. And, as far as relationships are concerned I think, personally, that in order for a relationship to last and work out, two people have to have a lot of respect and kindness toward one another.

I also think the two people need to realize that when they are arguing or having some sort of disagreement where two different viewpoints seem to clash and a problem doesn't seem to have a way to be resolved amicably, I think a lot of this has to do with keeping in mind that you're not fighting each other, but, rather, disagreeing about how to solve a problem. To be fair, there are many approaches and solutions that are likely viable usually. So you're not attacking each other, you're attacking the problem from different points of view.

All of this being said, let's turn our attention onto how the law of hypnosis can influence and impact relationships in a positive way.

Perhaps you're not at present in a relationship with someone or you've had relationship problems or you simply can't seem to get relationships right. If this happens to be you I think a lot of people are in your same boat; namely, having the same types of problems, struggles, and difficulties that you have had in the past and may still be having.

What can happen, and I've seen it happen often with many of my former therapy clients is that you can begin to entertain certain thought patterns, which in turn become beliefs that have you valuing relationships in a completely unhealthy way; preventing you and acting as an obstacle in your way, as far as finding and having the right life-partner to be with.

On a positive note, you can utilize the power of your 'hypnotic mind' to manifest into your life the right partner for you. This can first happen by annihilating any presumptions you may have entertained as a result of past experiences with relationships that have gone sour and not worked out as you would have liked for them to. Your past is your past. It isn't your future. It isn't your present.

As I mentioned in a previous chapter, people have a tendency to look at their past and draw certain conclusions about themselves and other people. Even about what is possible and what is not, due to what is referred to in psychology as 'classical conditioning' or 'respondent conditioning'.

What can happen is whenever you experience an opportunity to enter a new relationship with someone the past experiences you've had can trigger an anchor causing you to once again behave in a certain way, or be certain that you'll fail in this new relationship as you have in all your past ones.

This conditioning of your mind has been brought about from relationships you've known others to have, past relationships you've had, what you've heard on television and on the news, what you've read about in other books, what you've experienced watching Hollywood or Bollywood movies, and so on.

If it seems as though you can't get relationships right what I recommend you do first, before you try anything else, is take an assessment of your past relationship experiences and start to make a list of all the different conclusions you've draws whereas relationships are concerned.

In regards to values, people have a tendency to value what causes them to least amount of pain. If being without a life partner seems to you to make the most sense I would like for you to take a few moments to assess this value; in other words, this idea that you find most important as far as being alone, partner free, being more useful to you than being with a partner, where as you might perceive certain problems can surface.

When you expect a problem to happen or expect a certain result, your 'hypnotic mind' doesn't take this lightly. What it does in turn is take these thoughts and these ideas, your past experiences or memories, what you value most, and what you have come to believe about relationships in general, as well as what state of mind you enter into whenever you think about being a relationship with someone. All of these criteria are the same criteria that has been mentioned throughout this book in previous chapters, which all effect your ability to critically think; specifically, as it relates to your 'critical faculty'. Now, I've mentioned that your critical faculty is a woven matrix of these five things that have come to be as a result of your past thinking, your past experiences, what you value most, what you believe to be true, and where your state of mind is when you think about what it is you want and don't want.

Many people become fearful that they're not cut out for relationships. This is simply a suggestion or belief that they've come to believe and once again a belief isn't always necessarily true; it's only what you believe.

If you value relationships on one hand, yet another part of you devalues them thinking that they're more trouble than they're worth, then your 'hypnotic mind' will continue to bring to you the same problems you've faced in the past. If you want to get over this hurdle you might be faced with, the first thing you must do is take an assessment of where your thoughts are, your values are, your beliefs are, what you past has influenced you to believe, as well as how you feel when you think about relationships.

WHY CAN THE LAW OF HYPNOSIS HELP ME MANIFEST MY IDEAL RELATIONSHIP

There are a few things to consider in terms of why you might want to employ your 'hypnotic mind' using the same hypnotic process you've learnt in other chapters to bring about other things into your life, such as: (a) health, (b) business success, and (c) wealth.

The first thing you want to understand is that you need to put your intentions out there to your 'hypnotic mind'. This does not mean telling your 'hypnotic mind' every minute detail of everything you 'have to have' in a mate. Rather, it means expressing the intention that you want to find the person in your life that makes the most sense and whom you'll love, who is the right person for you. And let it happen.

You don't have to worry about how it's going to happen, just simply let it happen. Utilizing the power of your hypnotic mind through the use of self-hypnosis gives you the advantage of allowing all the 'parts' of you to come on board and really work together in sync to find you the 'right' person. Instead of only one aspect of your personality being allowed to decide the right mate for you, you'll now have all the 'aspects' of you focused in the right direction harmoniously so that they can all work together to create for you 'unconsciously' the right mate and someone you'll be able to share your life, good times with, and both be there for one another during the good times and the bad.

Of course, there won't be 'bad' times per se, since you'll be hypnotically creating the best life for yourselves. So just get the negative thoughts out of your mind and be prepared for the best, yet, to come in life!

The second thing you want to understand is that you need to have faith and positive expectancy that the right person is going to come along and sweep you off your feet. This means you don't want to doubt the process; rather, you want to trust that things are going to work out and that the 'right' person is going to come into your life at the 'right' time, in the 'right' way, and, essentially you want to have positive expectancy about this. You don't need to worry yourself to death about, "Am I going to be alone for the rest of my life?" You don't need to think about being with every person that comes along in your awareness. All you need to concern yourself with is having positive expectancy that everything is going to work itself out, the right person is out there and is being magnetized into your life, you're going to be happy, and you're not going to have to think about being with anybody else, because this person will be the 'right' person for you. You will also be the right person for them. Together you will both enjoy a wonderful life and be able to create great things together.

The third thing you want to understand is that you need to understand 'how' your 'hypnotic mind' operates.

Now, we've talked about this in past chapters. So this is really nothing new, but it is a good idea to keep yourself reminded of how the Law of Hypnosis works.

The first step, the first thing you want to do, is you want to put out there a focus on what it is you want to hypnotize into your life. Now this is paralleling the same process of inducing self-hypnosis in yourself, which is you simply stare at an object or a spot on the wall and you focus your attention completely on that spot. This is the same thing you're doing with manifesting the right mate into your life. You're putting your intention out there and focusing on just that intention. You're letting those thoughts override any negative thoughts, any doubts, any insecurities you may have, and you're simply allowing yourself to just be hyperfocused on having the right person in your life, and this person coming into your life at the perfect time. In the right way, also.

The second stage of manifesting using the Law of Hypnosis is simply to allow your mind to relax and allow things to come in. This also parallels the next step in the process of self-hypnosis, which is to suspend your disbelief and doubts, and to allow you guard to go down so that things can 'happen' to come about without any resistance or objections getting in the way. You don't have to reject things anymore; rather, you can start to accept things, and have faith in the things that are coming. In the same regard this is exactly what you are doing when you're attracting a 'mate' into your life. You're letting down your guard, you're allowing the right person to come in without all the negativities that come from old thought-patterns, old values you may have had that hindered you, old beliefs about how relationships have to work in order for you to be happy, past experiences you may have had in terms of people you've previously dated and the mark that they've left which has led you to form certain biases and opinions about what being in a relationship has to be, but remember: The past does not dictate the future. People don't get to where they are in life by continuing to experience the same things from the past, otherwise they would never get anywhere, and their past would continue to haunt them.

The last step in the process of using the Law of Hypnosis to manifest things into your life is to allow suggestions that are positive affirmations about what it is you want to be seeded into the fertile playground of your 'hypnotic mind'. This simply means knowing what it is you want, having the right thoughts, and as you go off into a deep hypnosis allowing those ideas to be planted there so that they can grow and mature and flower and blossom and self-express themselves in the external reality you live consciously in. Of course, this is just as we've said; that is, this is the same process used to hypnotize ourselves, which is where you allow yourself to go into a deep trance and you allow yourself to mentally 'think-on' and recite the desires of your heart, i.e. hypnotic suggestions, to your 'hypnotic mind'.

So now you are beginning to make some sense of what I said, when in the first chapter of this book, about why it is I call this the Law of Hypnosis instead of the Law of Attraction, like so many other people refer to it as. Also why I use terms like 'hypnotic mind' instead of 'subconscious mind' or 'unconscious mind'. Why I use 'mind' instead of saying 'conscious mind'. Because, now you are beginning to understand that the process of manifesting something into your life is exactly the same process as 'hypnotizing' something into your life. Hypnotizing yourself.

When you have an alignment with what it is you want in life, who you want to associate with, what type of income you want to generate, whether you want to operate a business, or not, whatever the case might be the Law of Hypnosis will bring to you exactly what you expect.

Therefore through positive expectancy and the process of self-hypnosis, I'm telling you that you can manifest anything into your life that you desire to have or to experience for the betterment of your life experience here on Earth.

The forth thing you want to understand is that you need to recognize when the right person comes along. This means don't reject everyone that shows up in our life; that is, we're keeping an open mind, allowing ourselves not to dismiss everyone as the 'wrong' person, but allowing ourselves not to judge, be too critical, and simply to accept that someone new has come into your life and now it's time to determine if it's the 'right' person or not.

What you don't want to start doing at this stage is to make judgments about the person who has come into your life. The only thing you need to concern yourself with is just maintaining the same innate intentions that you put out in step one: having positive attentions about the right person entering your life at the right time. That's it! If you can do 'that' you'll be on the right path to finding the right person before you even realize it.

Sometimes we don't always recognize the 'right' person when they come into our lives. Sometimes we easily dismiss people without giving them a chance. It is the same thing we do with new opportunities that we find ourselves confronted with making choices about. We have a tendency, because of past experiences, values, beliefs, thought-patterns, and state of mind, to discount experiences and people before we've given ourselves a chance to make a sound determination. Sometimes something that seems negative is actually not, and in fact can be the greatest blessing. You have to take care not to formulate opinions too early. Don't let outcomes dictate your state of mind or thought-patterns either. They will rob you of getting what it is you want. Take outcomes as they come, by remembering you have the 'hypnotic' powers inside you to change anything about your life—like a child playing on the playground, playing pretend with their playmates.

WHAT DO I NEED TO DO TO HYPNOTICALLY ATTRACT THE RIGHT MATE

Getting information before the fact instead of after is critical to finding the right mate, as it is in making the right decision that will satisfy all aspects of your personality and psychological makeup. For this reason it is imperative you keep a sound mind about you, while not limiting your choices. In this section we'll discuss a few things you need to know that will make attracting the right mate a much more enjoyable process.

What you need to understand first is that you need to recognize what you think you want isn't always what you want. Now, whenever something new comes into your life, and I'm not just talking relationships here, but anything; it could be an idea, or a suggestions, or a random thought. It may sound very exciting, and the person pitching the idea to you may be in a state of mind that causes you to change your state, and become magnetized to their ideal. And, this is something you have to be careful of, because it is easy, whenever someone throws something at you, for you to leash onto that idea as though it were right for you.

The truth is what we think we want or what we think sounds good to us isn't always in our best interest to acquire or experience. It isn't always going to be the thing that makes us happy. You see for this particular reason, having a sound understanding and recognition of what it is that's right for you upfront can be a litmus test by which you discern whether something is right for you or it's not. If things are not lining up like the stars for you whereas relationships are concerned there is probably a good reason for it. You need to recognize that what you want is best defined by understanding the parts of you and noting the ones in conflict with one another.

Let me give an example. You might be faced with someone new in your life. This person may be really attractive, may have a vibrant personality, upon other impressive attributes; however, there may be certain things about this person that simply don't jive well with who and what you are as a human being. For example, they might have a different belief system and outlook on how life should be lived, they may have different values that conflict with yours, and they may even have a past history that leaves them carrying baggage that you don't want to take on were you to be in a relationship with them. These are all things that at first you might not recognize or consider and later on could come and pose a relationship problem. For this reason it is important to take an in depth assessment about what it is you want, not just in terms of looks, and other superficial attributes; rather, observe in your mind how your days would be spent with this person, and not just on a rare day, where excitement and pleasure revive the experience of being with them, but a 'common' day. What does a common day look like for you spending with this person? Are they going to meet your expectations as far as upkeep on a house, or an environment you happen to be in? Will they be able to be in the same environment as you prefer? Will you be able to live in the same environment as them and what their preferences and needs are?

So these are practical things that you can do ahead of time before you begin the manifesting process utilizing the Law of Hypnosis so that you can prepare the path ahead of time. This will also help you 'hypnotic mind' weed-out things that aren't going to work for you so that it will more precisely bring into your life the right person for you.

The second thing you need to understand is that you must have a 'knowing' the right person is out there seeking you just as fervently as you are seeking them. This is a dimension of the Law of Hypnosis that you must understand, before embarking hypnotically to manifest someone into your life. This begins with you; that is, how badly do you want someone in your life? How much do you care if someone is in your life or not? Are you 'willy-nilly'? Is it, "Okay, I'll take it or leave it"? Because, understanding this is going to drastically increase how quickly someone comes into your life that is the 'right' person. This person is seeking you, just as much as you're seeking them out.

So it's about intensity. It's about the level of desire you have to be with the right person, and the stronger that grow in you, the stronger that desire grows in that perfect match for you.

Keep these things in mind, when hypnotically attracting a mate. More than this though, these are sound principles that need to be understood when it comes to hypnotically attracting 'anything' into your life.

You may be the type of person who wants to attract a brand new car. You have an idea of what the car should look like, and so you put into motion the hypnotic principles of attraction; however, maybe you're not as onboard whereas intensity and excitement are concerned about having a new car, because you're weighing the negatives from past purchases. Maybe the idea of making payments doesn't set well with you. Maybe the price tag is a turn-off. It could be many or a combination of factors that don't have you 'turned-on' about getting the car, and so you're less emotionally excited as someone else who 'really' wants that particular vehicle to be driving. These things leave you, instead, thinking: "If it happens, it happens; if it doesn't, it doesn't."

I'm here to tell you that this type of thinking (stinking thinking) is the same type of thinking that isn't going to get you they type of car that you want. It isn't going to get hypnotically manifested into your life. And, as strange as this may sound, the truth is: As badly as you want that car is as badly as that car wants you.

Is there a care out there for you? You bet you! However, you have to want what you want with fervency if you want what you want to want you.

So having a 'knowing' that the right person is out there for you is one thing, but you have to want and 'really' want this person in your life if you can expect to bring this person in.

What you need to understand thirdly is that you need to realize what's worked for you in the past—hasn't worked! The relationships you've entertained in the past that you thought were right for you at the time haven't worked out so well, have they?

I know this may be a little 'heavy' and it may be a little difficult to relent to agreeing with me on, and perhaps you downright don't like me right now, but you need to admit openly without judgment that what's worked for you in the past, hasn't worked. For this reason you need to be open to new possibilities and new people and different types of new personalities coming into your life to bring in joy, happiness, and amazements that you can share intimately with another person.

The preconceived notions you've had from your past experiences don't let them drive down the probability that you'll have success, happiness, and prosperity in your next relationship. To do so would be a mistake I feel.

The past is the past. Good, bad, or indifferent—doesn't matter! The past is the past. If you think someone from your past is someone who is going to be in your future maybe there's nothing wrong with that; however, let me suggest that thinking this way is limiting the opportunities out there for you to experience a real chance to meet someone exactly right for you. Be open.

You can't use the Law of Hypnosis to bring someone into your life who's clearly not the right person for you, because the relationship will not be lasting. You'll have to go through repercussions and consequences you don't want to experience, and you'll probably hate me so much for your bad fortune that you'll probably burn this book and curse me (just kidding).

What you need to understand lastly is that you don't need to blame or judge yourself. You don't need to blame or judge yourself about poor decisions you've made in the past and the unenjoyable experiences that resulted. Circumstances as bizarre as they may have been—it doesn't matter—don't blame or judge yourself! Look at these as merely 'feedback' which is a resourceful way of getting to where you want to be from where you've been.

Personal blame and judgments lead to places you don't want to traverse. You'll hypnotically attract the wrong things back into your life to punish yourself. You have to change this thinking so that you manifest into your life the best life possible for yourself using the Law of Hypnosis.

There are all the things you need to understand first before hypnotizing someone into your life that is the 'right' person for you.

HOW DO I USE THE LAW OF HYPNOSIS TO FALL IN LOVE

Falling in love is a hypnotic experience. Often people find themselves losing focus of practicalities whereas logic and reason are concerned and entering the playfully hypnotic world of make believe and pretend. We can understand someone on a level nobody else can when we're interlocked together in what we call 'love'.

We use the world 'love' as though it's a real tangible object. Love is a word that has been nominalized from the action verb 'to love'. 'To love' seems somehow more fleeting as though at any moment the act of loving someone might end, without notice. The word 'love' on the other hand is concrete and permanent. This makes 'love' lasting and eternal, and something we value as priceless in terms of the experience.

Now here's the deal: you can use the Law of Hypnosis to manifest your own hypnotic love story into reality. Meaning, you can harness the power of your 'hypnotic mind' to hypnotize love to you. It is as simple as taking a magnet to a bag of metal bolts. The bolts stick magnetically to the magnet.

The process for hypnotically magnetizing love into your life is no different than what you would do to hypnotize anything else into your life; such as: (a) wealth, (b) business success, and (c) health, and so on. When it comes to love, however, because it is a concept and not something that you can perceive objectively, I feel it is a good idea to first take out a sheet of paper and a pencil and just jot down some of the things you're looking for in terms of a relationship. These things should be relative to your conceptualization of what love is, because everybody has a different conception of what love means to them. There are some beautiful poetic verses that have been written throughout history that have been inspired by peoples' ideas of what love should be. These are love inspired. So it may be a good idea for you to connect with some of this first and get some inspiration inside your heart to give you some sort of 'grounding' or 'reference point' regarding what love means to you.

So you might want to ink down some thoughts about love first. These different ideas will take you closer into a communion with your concept of what love is. It will also help you attach some feelings to these thoughts. This will put you into a perfect state of mind for hypnotically manifesting the love of your life into your life.

The first thing you want to do to hypnotically magnetize love into your life using the Law of Hypnosis is to start with an extreme desire and focus. This is your intent to manifest a real love story into your life. This is you stepping up to the plate and firmly and resoundingly sounding the fanfare trumpets to alert your hypnotic mind that you desire romance and love in your life.

When you do this you want to be in compliant state with what you know you must do to get what you want. This means not being afraid of letting your 'hypnotic mind' have control and power to act to bring about what it is you desire and say you want. You also want all the aspects of your personality and tendencies on board with this decision. It's a commitment. Once you commit to buy into this process there's no refunds—you're going to manifest love into your life by some means. We're temperamental creatures, with a tendency to be wishy-washy and flighty, but once you make this vow to yourself, this promise, then you must see it through and remain focused and intent to have it. If you don't you won't get what your heart desires.

Once everything is congruent with all the parts of yourself in terms of what you want, and you begin to zero in and focus your attention 100% on passion and love and your desire to find the right person for you, what you'll start to find is that your 'hypnotic mind' become prepped for the next step.

So the second thing you want to do to hypnotically magnetize love into your life using the Law of Hypnosis is to bypass the critical faculty.

Now you've helped this step along already simply making a declaration to yourself in every way that this is something that you want. Yet, what tends to happen for some of us is some of the old conditioned thought patterns start to creep in and tell you differently. They start to feed you lessons from your past that might not have been so pleasant as far as relationships were concerned, and so the nature of this critical faculty then is to test your faith, and test how onboard you focus and intent really is in order that you might receive a hypnotic manifestation from your hypnotic mind.

This is testing the water, so don't be afraid when you start to encounter some resistance and red-flags or start to rethink your decision making stance, or start to find yourself falling into a different state of mind that is incongruent with how you should be feeling in order to achieve what you want from your hypnotic mind, as these are all perfectly normal things people go through from time to time; however, this second step does required that you bypass all that thinking, those negative states, past experiences, old believes that no longer work for you anymore, old things you may have in the past valued, but which are no longer important, and in doing so keep a strong state of mind that is conducive and which supports your desire to find love and happiness in your life.

Once you've accomplished this step, which is really ways the most difficult for most people, you're then ready to move onto step number three.

The third thing you want to do to hypnotically magnetize love into your life using the Law of Hypnosis is to actually stimulate your 'hypnotic mind'.

So backtracking for a moment: You've echoed what it is you want. You've decided that finding love is the most important thing for you at this time in your life. It is now an obsession of sorts. You're emotionally fixated on this idea of love and finding it. You've gotten tunnel vision from such extreme focus on this lofty aspiration. Then in the process of examination you start to logically reflect on other things that could out of sync with these ideas and bypass them to keep your intent and focus maintained and without question.

Now it's time to stimulate the 'hypnotic mind'. This requires you to quieten your mind. Enter a deep state of hypnosis using self-hypnosis techniques taught throughout this book. Allow yourself to relax and trance out completely. Be in a state of hypnosis in which you're aware of everything; yet, not aware of anything. When you achieve this state you can then feel love inside your being and reminisce on your conception of love, using picture, feelings, and metaphors to communicate to your hypnotic mind. When you do this you'll find that you feel as though you are in the right place, it's the right time, and the world is your domain.

This is the same state a child enters using his/her creative faculty to play pretend and make believe whatever they like into form. These formative years for some are the best years of our lives. This is what stimulating the 'hypnotic mind' all is about. It's about dissociating yourself from limitations and what's not possible, and realizing in a special moment that anything is possible and the world is one infinite playground to create whatever you want. You know in this state of being that you're in the right place and what you want you are going to hypnotically attract without doubt or uncertainty.

After achieving this you're then ready to communicate and talk to your 'hypnotic mind' to actually assert to it what it is you want from it. This means seeding suggestions to it.

The last thing you want to do to hypnotically magnetize love into your life using the Law of Hypnosis is to plant your desire and get you 'knowing' and be transported off into the fire-pit of creation where everything you want comes true.

By planting desires you want to tell your 'hypnotic mind' through your emotions, thoughts, pictures, and all the methods you might want to use to communicate with your hypnotic mind hypnotically to express all the things you earlier had written down on paper, which involves love, what you want in a relationship, and how you see your life being as a result of getting what you want.

By doing this you have now completed the last step of manifesting your own love story into your life. Really, at this point the only thing left to do is have the expectation that what you want is coming about. And, so as you come back to your everyday reality you'll normally feel a calmness that comes over you and this calm sensation is very peaceful and really the first indication that what you've wanted to hypnotically manifest into your life has been established as a seed of possibility. Now, while you wait for the right relationship to come along and someone to sweep you off your feet just become observant of the external reality around you. You may notice that you start to come into some bizarre situations that are outside your normal patterns of existing. You may find yourself eating at a different restaurant one day. You may find yourself driving home from work and the road being shut down and you'll have to detour somewhere. These are all things that we take for granted and assume are random acts. I'm here to tell you that they're not random. They are all the roads being laid down before you by your 'hypnotic mind' to help you get the object of your affection.

WHAT IF I WANT TO MANIFEST OTHER TYPES OF RELATIONSHIPS INTO MY LIFE

Not only can you manifest a significant other, you can also manifest healthy friendships, parental bonds, and really a strong relationship with people you truly care about and who truly care about you.

The sky truly is the limit in terms of what types of relationships, experiences, and objects you can manifest into your reality. This truly should inspire you, uplift you, and give you hope about your future—you can accomplish anything using the Law of Hypnosis.

You see, one of the saddest things a person can do, in my opinion, is not live to their full potential and not experience the things in life worth living. Even relationships need nourishing and work from time to time. However, using the Law of Hypnosis you can begin to start formulating relationships that are lasting, impactful, helpful, and one that you will cherish for the rest of your life.

I remember back in 2008, I had just returned home from a trainer's training workshop I was giving in India, and the economy at the time was spiraling downward out of control, the housing market had burst, there were government bailouts of some of the nation's largest banks, and Lehman Brothers and Bear Sterns did in fact go belly up. This country was having some real financial issues. The times were trying at best, and it seemed to me that overnight many people had seemed to lose their hope and their inner strength.

This was something I perceived as a collective depression that was affecting the vast majority. It was a bleak observation to learn that some of the strongest people in my life and most financially well-off were fearful and afraid and not the same people I had known just a few years earlier.

A part of me wanted to wake them up—to shake them out of this oblivion. I couldn't though, and this left me feeling inwardly depressed and somewhat detached from people.

Ever since I experience all this negativity and watched those I loved the most experience hardships that were hard to wrap my mind around, I knew I wanted to write this book and share this information with others.

I used this very information I'm sharing with you to help nurse wounded relationship, and create healthy new relationships that I suspect will remain intact for the rest of my life. You can literally take any relationship and manifest it back to health. You can.

Getting back to manifesting other types of relationships for a moment: I know you can take this information and not only manifest that all your relationships be healthy and rewarding in the ways you desire for them to be, but I know you can the information in this book and hypnotically manifest everything you want out of life.

The system is the same easy system I've taught you throughout this entire book: (a) focus on what you want, (b) suspend your disbelief and doubt, (c) attach strong emotions, while you're hypnotized, to what you want to hypnotically attract, (d) talk to your hypnotic mind as though it were a wishing well going to fulfill your every wish, by giving it your hypnotic suggestions, and (e) start to notice immediate changes happening in your life that are pulling to you what it is you desire.

It really is this simple. It doesn't take much time for you to do, and the payoff is a richly rewarding life that you can feel astonished by.

CHAPTER NOTES

So to recap this chapter, we start off my having a discussion about basic civility and being king one to another in a relationship. When two people are together and they're arguing or having an argument about something, it is important they realize they're not fighting against each other, they're actually attacking a problem from different sides and perspective.

Beyond this, however, and directed to the person who happens to be single or in a relationship going no-where, an alternative can be that you use the Law of Hypnosis to manifest your ideal relationship. Now, this strategy is no different from any of the other strategies I've listed throughout this book. The only difference here is that we're now looking at something not tangible and not necessarily an 'experience'; but, rather, a relationship. This is a partnership where two people get together and decide to be together, or spend time together romantically.

You want to be with the 'right' person so you're not worst off than you would be were you by yourself, or with someone altogether different.

The astonishing thing about using hypnosis to attract the right mate to you is that you understand and recognize what you think you want isn't always what you want. Sometimes we have the best intentions and think we know everything and we think we know what's best for us; yet, sometimes this is only one aspect or a fraction of our holistic-self speaking to us and giving us ideas that turn into thought-patterns. As a result we start to believe certain things and it's not necessarily true. There is this holistic side to our humanity that needs to be taken into consideration. Who's right for you for all of who you are, in every aspect? You want someone who respects you and gives you the time of day. You also want to be with someone that you deeply care about and who reciprocates this caring back onto you.

You need to understand that when you're with someone you want them to be just as attracted to you as you are attracted to them. Attraction isn't always looks either! Attraction is the whole person. You can use this Law of Hypnosis to really help guide you in finding the right person for yourself. You can use your 'hypnotic mind' to weed out things that aren't going to work for you. This can be as simple as using plain commonsense sometimes; but, by adding the hypnotic element to this process you take away a lot of the critical thinking aspects to allow deeper parts of you to emerge and have a say. It is one thing to critically analyze everything, quite another to take into consideration your feelings, emotions, and other parts of you not often given a chance to be heard because you operate so much of the time critically, ignoring these other sides to you.

We also looked at how to make it possible for ourselves to use the Law of Hypnosis to find love, fall in love, and be in a relationship founded on kindness and respect for one another. Too, we looked at how love can be observed from its linguistic aspect as being something tangible, and easy to grasp onto and perceive. Yet, we also discussed how love comes from the action 'to love' which is much more fluid and less static in terms of how it's perceived. When you think of the word 'loving' and equate it with an action verb: we're loving to do this; we're loving someone; and so on, it's easy to see love as fluid and not so static. The more static word 'love' has a more infinite connotation to it. When we say to someone, "I love you," it really is meant in such a way this love is a bond between you and I, and its forever.

Frequently, today, in our society 'love' the word itself can be used cliché. People say, "I love you," all the time; yet, it's almost a surface type of love with no depth to it. Pertaining to taking a relationship forward or hypnotizing the right relationship into your reality there are a number of steps you can take; notably, these steps happen not to be any different than manifesting anything else into your life. It simply requires you to focus on your desire, making it a priority. The thing you focus on is what you care about and what's important to you. Once something becomes important to you certain emotions start come about as a result. These emotions are interpreted by your 'hypnotic mind' the same way 'words' and 'language' are interpreted by your critical thinking 'mind'. More than this they create motivation inside of you to want to achieve and gain what it is you want out of life. This can help you stay tied to your goals, which in turn helps to bring them about.

This process is the same that you would use self-hypnosis for in curing a phobia, a habit, or something holding you back from success. You simply want to focus your attention somewhere. It doesn't have to be on the goal, per se, it can be that you focus on something meaningless to you, like some object or spot on a wall; however, by focusing your attention internally hypnosis is achieved much more rapidly and from my experiences works more effectively to help you get what you want faster.

This internal focus will help you then slip into an 'alpha' state which is a hypnotic state in which you are suggestible.

From here you can implant hypnotic suggestions that you want your 'hypnotic mind' to remedy or create as an externality in your life—one you can experience with your five senses.

Once you deliver hypnotic suggestions to your 'hypnotic mind' you can simply be on the lookout for things to start shifting subtly or even rapidly sometimes in your life. You'd be surprised how often people's lives change and morph suddenly once they put hypnosis to work for them in manifesting their needs, desires, and dreams.

ACTION STEPS

The following action steps are meant to help you think about what you want, to bring about what you think. Please do the exercises even if you've done them before in the past on some other course. Your compliance is evidence of your real desire to manifest outwardly what you most seek, desire, and dream of having, experiencing, and achieving in life.

I. Make yourself take stock of what you think you want in a relationship. There are two ways to accomplish this: (a) be general about what it is you want in a mate, and (b) be very specific about what it is you want in a mate. Rank order both lists; that is, the general list, and the specific list. Next, take your specifics and subsection them underneath where they fall at in your 'general' categories list.

II. Hypnotize yourself using the self-hypnosis protocol in this book and seed your desires in a mate into your 'hypnotic mind'. Do this often, and every day, ensuring you do not do anything that will block your success in finding the mate of your dreams.

III. Journal your experiences day-by-day and record 'out of the blue' coincidences that start to come about. This is to help you keep your 'knowing' that your 'hypnotic mind' is working in 'mysterious' ways to bring about the life you desire. When the 'right' mate comes into your life you then 'know' it and it will not be any shock to you. Remember, keep an expectancy for positives to show up in your life and they will, I promise.

CHAPTER 8

POSTSCRIPT

The end of the book. This is where things really get interesting, because in one sense it's your time to shine. By now, hopefully you've implemented some of the activities at the end of the chapters to start manifesting some things, experiences, and relationships into your life.

During the test phase when I taught a workshop on the 'Law of Hypnosis' I brought together a group of ten individuals and let them suspend their disbelief and doubt in order to be test participants in using this information.

I can share with great success how these individuals, though their levels of success varied, mostly due to their differences regarding needs, desires, and dreams, were with great astonishment upon hypnotizing into their lives exactly what they wanted. To see their faces light up with bright smiles was fantastic, and one more reason I knew somewhere deep inside of me I wanted to write this book.

The weightiest handicap we have as human beings is our own thinking. It's the limitations we place on ourselves that make us think, feel, believe, value, and act a certain way. We all think we have all the answers by justifying logically the reasons why. The truth is deeper than your logic, and when you push logic to the side, not to say that logic doesn't have a place or value, you start to allow in incredibly hypnotic momentum burst into wonderment and creativity and get you real results. Actually, not just 'real' result, but the 'best' result possible. Results, in fact, that you wouldn't have been able to logically perceive on your best day.

This mental handicap we find ourselves facing is really just an illusion. It is an illusion placed before us by the conditioning of society, by the way we grew up believing things should be. When we stopped realizing that anything is possible if we'll only believe it's possible, value it, think it, and wish it into our life through the intensity of our state of mind; similar, to a child wishing a 'make-believe' to come true, we started putting obstacles, ones which weren't there, in our way, which prevented us from getting our wishes fulfilled.

My ultimate hope is that you'll take this information and apply it. I'm not asking you to get immediately get excited and gung-ho on the prospect of getting whatever it is in life you want. I realize there are a lot of people who have a 'Doubting Thomas' hiding inside them. They don't like to give into the possibility that other possibilities are possible—I get it. This is fine and even in many ways understandable from a logically critical perspective.

My true goal for you is to have you bring into your life exactly what it is you want; that is, to bring it in, in a way that is beneficial to you, as well as the other people in your life.

If you happen to be a small business owner and you find yourself working around the clock, all the time, and without much reward for your labors, then if you take what I'm suggestion you do as outlined in this book, and implement it, you'll find that solutions come in, as well as answers you've been hoping for, and without any effort on your part. It will seem like too easy an approach. You'll at first rationalize that it can't be this simple. I assure you, from my own experiences, and those of others I've worked closes with to learn this law that it is exactly this simple. It only requires, again, that you suspend your doubt in it being this easy.

If you find yourself in and out of relationships, never making any of them work, wishing like mad that you could simply wave a magic wand and have your soul-mate or perfect partner, then I'm here to tell you that you can take the information in this book and use the 'Law of Hypnosis' to manifest this person to you. Remember as you do, however, that the person you're seeking is seeking you just as passionately. Using hypnosis and remaining single-mindedly focused on attracting the right person in will come about in the most mysterious ways—yet, you can be assured—it will happen.

All you need to do to observe logically that this law works is to notice how like groups of people gather in like locations. New Yorkers get stereotyped as New Yorkers with having their hard attitudes, etc. Not to stereotype or judge ever New Yorker as having a hard attitude. Californians are likewise stereotyped by their liberal, laid-back personalities; yet, not every Californian is liberal or laidback. You get the point though, which is that 'like attracts like'. You see wealthy people associating with other wealthy people. You see poor people associating with other poor people. Families associating with other families. Business executives associating with other business executives. Etc. Etc.

You have to know you have a critical mind that outright rejects foreign ideas and things it does not associate with as logical. This is why some people believe one way and others another. It's your conditioning. I'm asking you to dissociate from it for a short while to attain what you want out of life. Plain and simple.

You also have a 'hypnotic mind' that gets things in pictures and feelings—for example, just consider these two statements: (a) "The baby burned to death in the fire," and (b) "The infant perished in the conflagration". Both of these sentences say, logically, exactly the same thing; however, our 'hypnotic mind' feels a stronger associated connection to the words: baby, burned, and fire. This is because as children these were the words first taught us until much later in life our vocabularies expanded to learn more synonyms that say the same things. These earlier emotional associations connect on a much deeper level with our 'hypnotic minds' than do the other words.

Whenever you want to attract something, someone, or an experience into your life all you must remember is this process that's outlined in this book. This is your instruction book; that is, this book is the bible on the 'Hypnotic Mind' and the 'Law of Hypnosis'.

BIBLIOGRAPHY

Assaraf, J. (2007). *Having it all: Achieving your life's goals and dreams* (Rev. ed.). New York: Atria Books.

Assaraf, J., & Smith, M. (2008). *The answer: Grow any business, achieve financial freedom, and live an extraordinary life.* New York: Atria Books.

Behrend, G., & Vitale, J. (2005). *How to attain your desires: How to live life and love it.* New York: Morgan James Pub.

Canfield, J., Mark Victor Hansen, Rogerson, M., Rutte, M., & Clauss, T. (n.d.). *Chicken soup for the soul at work: 101 stories of courage, compassion, and creativity in the workplace.*

Chopra, D. (1995). *The way of the wizard: Twenty spiritual lessons in creating the life you want.* New York: Harmony Books.

Chopra, D. (1997). *The path to love: Renewing the power of spirit in your life.* New York: Harmony Books.

Chopra, D. (2003). *The spontaneous fulfillment of desire: Harnessing the infinite power of coincidence.* New York: Harmony Books.

Dyer, W. W. (1989). *You'll see it when you believe it.* New York: W. Morrow.

Dyer, W. W. (1997). *Manifest your destiny: The nine spiritual principles for getting everything you want.* New York: HarperCollins.

Dyer, W. W. (2008). *Living the wisdom of the Tao: The complete Tao te ching and affirmations.* Carlsbad, Calif.: Hay House.

Dyer, W. W. (2009). *No excuses!: How what you say can get in your way.* Carlsbad, Calif.: Hay House.

Dyer, W. W. (2010). *The power of intention: Learning to co-create your world your way.* Carlsbad, Calif.: Hay House, Inc.

Erickson, M. H., & Rossi, E. L. (1979). *Hypnotherapy: An exploratory casebook.* New York, NY: Irvington Publishers.

Ledochowski, I. (2003). *The deep trance training manual.* Carmarthen, Wales; Williston, VT: Crown House Pub.

Losier, M. J. (2007). *Law of attraction: The science of attracting more of what you want and less of what you don't.* New York: Wellness Central.

Losier, M. J. (2009). *Law of connection* (pp. 24, 33, and 43). New York and Boston: Wellness Central.

Murphy, J. (1963). *The power of your subconscious mind*. Englewood Cliffs, N.J.: Prentice-Hall.

Murphy, J. (1966). *Your infinite power to be rich*. West Nyack, N.Y.: Parker Pub. Co.

Murphy, J. (1973). *Telepsychics: The magic power of perfect living*. West Nyack, N.Y.: Parker Pub. Co.

Murphy, J. (2001). *Think yourself rich: Use the power of your subconscious mind to find true wealth*. Paramus, NJ: Reward Books.

Murphy, J. (2002). *Think yourself to health, wealth &; Happiness: The best of Joseph Murphy's cosmic wisdom*. New York: Reward.

Norman Vincent Peale. (1987). *The power of positive thinking* (Special 35th anniversary ed.). New York: Prentice Hall Press.

Proctor, B. (2008). *The science of getting rich: Power priciples for creating more wealth in a rapidly changing world*. Retrieved from http://www.seminarsondvd.com

Richard, W. (2004). *Principles of behavior* (5th ed.). Upper Saddle River, N.J.: Pearson/Prentice Hall.

Smart, J. (2013). *Clarity: Clear mind, better performance, bigger results*. Chichester: Capstone.

Vitale, J. (1998). *There's a customer born every minute: P.T. Barnum's secrets to business success.* New York: AMACOM.

Vitale, J. (2005). *The attractor factor: 5 easy steps for creating wealth (or anything else) from the inside out.* Hoboken, N.J.: J. Wiley.

Vitale, J. (2006). *There's a customer born every minute: P.T. Barnum's amazing 10 "rings of power" for creating fame, fortune, and a business empire today--guaranteed.* Hoboken, N.J.: John Wiley.

Vitale, J. (2007). *Hypnotic writing: How to seduce and persuade customers with only your words.* Hoboken, N.J.: John Wiley & Sons.

Westra, B. (2013). *NLP and hypnosis: Influence and persuasions patterns.* Murray, KY: Indirect Knowledge Limited.

INDEX

achieving, 14, 23, 34, 37, 39, 43, 44, 47, 49, 59, 60, 69, 70, 71, 76, 97, 98, 99, 120, 128
alert, 4, 5, 6, 7, 8, 16, 38, 117
Alpha, 6
asleep, 5, 7, 8, 11, 17
aspect, 8, 14, 76, 105, 125, 126
assess, 14, 15, 50, 103
attention, 11, 17, 22, 73, 75, 92, 102, 106, 118, 127
attitude, 9, 30, 44, 134
aware, 6, 15, 24, 29, 47, 52, 63, 71, 89, 120
Beliefs, 15
believe, 2, 4, 9, 13, 14, 15, 18, 19, 20, 21, 26, 27, 29, 32, 35, 40, 42, 43, 48, 50, 63, 65, 67, 74, 77, 81, 82, 84, 85, 92, 103, 104, 116, 120, 125, 132, 134, 138
Beta, 5

Bob Proctor, 2
brain, 3, 4, 5, 23, 28, 63
Bypass the Critical Faculty, 17
chants, 11
communicating, 7, 11, 12, 19, 20, 21, 24, 91
communing, 12
conceive, 13, 27
conceptual, 2, 5, 7
consciously, 3, 7, 8, 16, 47, 52, 63, 71, 72, 93, 98, 108
contagious, 16, 17
critical faculty, 14, 17, 20, 22, 31, 91, 92, 104, 118
critical thinking, 4, 5, 11, 13, 19, 22, 35, 63, 67, 68, 85, 125, 127
cults, 11
Current State, 16
cycles, 6, 13
Delta, 8
desire, 2, 8, 9, 12, 13, 23, 26, 29, 32, 34, 37, 39,

40, 44, 45, 48, 49, 54, 55, 58, 59, 73, 76, 77, 83, 84, 85, 88, 92, 98, 99, 109, 113, 117, 118, 119, 120, 123, 124, 126, 128, 129, 137
disbelief, 9, 19, 107, 123, 131
distraction, 18
dream, 1, 23, 37, 44, 59, 72, 76, 83, 98, 99, 128
Earl Nightingale, 2
education, 13, 68
emotional, 4, 5, 12, 23, 75, 90, 98, 100, 134
escape, 12
expect, 3, 51, 75, 92, 93, 103, 108, 114
expectations, 13, 112
experience, 6, 7, 8, 12, 13, 20, 27, 34, 39, 40, 43, 47, 49, 50, 51, 52, 56, 71, 72, 73, 74, 77, 87, 103, 107, 109, 111, 112, 115, 116, 122, 123, 124, 127, 134
experimenting, 3
explicit, 11
external reality, 2, 7, 31, 108, 121

faith, 9, 40, 90, 97, 105, 107, 118
fantasizing, 7
feeling, 11, 16, 24, 34, 51, 67, 73, 87, 92, 98, 119, 123
feelings, 22, 23, 87, 98, 117, 120, 125, 134
Focus Attention, 17
focused, 3, 5, 47, 49, 51, 71, 75, 89, 97, 105, 118, 133
focusing, 11, 56, 57, 61, 107, 127
habitual thoughts, 15, 91
have, 1, 2, 3, 7, 8, 9, 11, 13, 14, 15, 17, 18, 20, 21, 22, 23, 24, 27, 29, 30, 31, 32, 35, 36, 37, 38, 40, 44, 47, 48, 49, 50, 51, 52, 55, 57, 59, 60, 62, 63, 64, 66, 68, 69, 70, 73, 74, 77, 79, 81, 82, 83, 84, 85, 86, 87, 89, 90, 91, 92, 95, 96, 97, 98, 99, 101, 102, 103, 105, 107, 108, 109, 110, 111, 112, 113, 114, 115, 117, 118, 119, 121,

125, 127, 132, 133, 134, 149
hyperfocus, 6
hyperfocusing, 11
hypnosis, 7, 11, 12, 13, 16, 17, 18, 19, 22, 24, 34, 35, 37, 40, 54, 55, 56, 57, 58, 64, 66, 67, 68, 71, 72, 75, 76, 84, 85, 91, 92, 93, 94, 98, 99, 102, 105, 106, 107, 108, 109, 120, 125, 127, 128, 133, 140
hypnotic mind, 5, 6, 12, 13, 17, 19, 20, 23, 24, 28, 31, 32, 34, 37, 38, 40, 42, 54, 66, 68, 71, 73, 74, 77, 84, 85, 88, 90, 91, 92, 93, 99, 100, 105, 108, 119, 120, 121, 134
hypnotic state, 6, 22, 52, 76, 127
hypnotize, 17, 19, 22, 106, 108, 116
hypnotizing, 19, 23, 70, 71, 108, 115, 126, 131
idea, 2, 8, 18, 20, 30, 31, 33, 42, 49, 50, 53, 55, 65, 69, 73, 75, 103, 106, 110, 113, 116, 119
imagination, 6, 91
imagining, 6, 19
immediacy, 3
impressionable, 13
induce, 22
influence, 15, 22, 64, 102
insights, 4, 6, 7, 59, 64, 66, 68, 69, 70, 71, 72, 75, 76
instructions, 4, 19, 43
intangible, 9, 27
Jack Canfield, 2
James Allen, 2
job, 13, 31, 38, 87, 93
Joe Vitale, 2
Joseph Murphy, 2, 139
journey, 9, 43
language, 4, 12, 19, 22, 94, 95, 98, 100, 126
Law of Attraction, 2, 3, 25, 108
Law of Hypnosis, 1, 53, 63, 64, 65, 66, 72, 73, 74, 75, 82, 83, 84, 85, 88, 89, 90, 91, 96, 97, 106, 107, 108, 112, 115, 116, 117, 118, 119, 120, 122, 124,

125, 126, 131, 133, 135, 149
leap of faith, 9
Like attracts like, 2, 41, 96
manifest, 1, 7, 21, 23, 31, 32, 34, 37, 38, 39, 40, 42, 43, 44, 45, 47, 48, 49, 50, 52, 53, 57, 58, 59, 63, 64, 65, 76, 84, 88, 89, 90, 92, 95, 96, 97, 99, 102, 108, 109, 112, 115, 116, 117, 118, 121, 122, 123, 124, 128, 133
Memories, 15
mental, 12, 20, 23, 37, 38, 51, 53, 54, 57, 58, 60, 63, 77, 132
method, 3, 9, 98
mind, 1, 2, 3, 4, 5, 6, 7, 8, 11, 12, 13, 14, 17, 19, 20, 21, 22, 24, 27, 28, 29, 31, 32, 33, 34, 35, 36, 37, 38, 39, 40, 42, 43, 44, 48, 49, 50, 51, 52, 53, 54, 55, 58, 59, 62, 64, 66, 67, 68, 70, 71, 73, 74, 75, 76, 77, 81, 82, 83, 84, 85, 86, 88, 89, 90, 91, 92, 93, 94, 95, 96, 97, 98, 99, 100, 101, 102, 103, 104, 105, 106, 107, 108, 109, 110, 112, 113, 116, 117, 118, 119, 120, 121, 123, 125, 126, 127, 128, 129, 132, 134, 139
mindful, 5, 12, 90
mindlessly, 8
minds, 3, 4, 33, 35, 36, 134
money, 1, 21, 29, 41, 56, 79, 80, 82, 83, 84, 86, 87, 88, 89, 90, 91, 96, 99
monotone, 17
Napoleon Hill, 2
need, 1, 13, 23, 30, 34, 36, 37, 41, 58, 59, 62, 68, 79, 84, 88, 89, 90, 94, 101, 105, 106, 109, 110, 111, 112, 113, 114, 115, 122, 125, 133
Norman Vincent Peale, 2
open minded, 13
patterns, 15, 17, 20, 28, 29, 30, 31, 32, 33, 34, 35, 36, 37, 39, 41, 48,

50, 52, 56, 63, 71, 73, 74, 81, 84, 88, 91, 92, 97, 100, 102, 107, 109, 118, 121, 125, 140
picture, 21, 24, 34, 43, 95, 120
pictures, 6, 12, 20, 21, 23, 68, 95, 121, 134
plan, 13, 59
ponder, 14
positive, 13, 26, 32, 33, 34, 35, 36, 40, 44, 47, 51, 52, 53, 56, 57, 58, 61, 62, 65, 72, 73, 90, 95, 98, 100, 102, 105, 108, 109
pretend, 6, 13, 19, 20, 110, 116, 120
principles, 3, 53, 88, 113, 138
process, 11, 17, 19, 20, 22, 26, 38, 39, 42, 43, 52, 54, 58, 63, 67, 70, 91, 92, 93, 94, 97, 105, 106, 107, 108, 109, 110, 112, 116, 118, 119, 125, 127, 135
quieting, 11
reality, 2, 4, 7, 12, 19, 21, 38, 40, 43, 80, 84, 94, 95, 97, 116, 121, 122, 126
receptive, 7
reject, 7, 14, 16, 33, 91, 107, 109
rejecting, 18, 92
religions, 11
Repetition, 11
repetitious, 11
repetitive, 18
results, 9, 38, 40, 41, 42, 53, 63, 64, 65, 67, 69, 70, 73, 74, 75, 82, 90, 98, 132, 139
rhythms, 6, 13
state, 5, 6, 7, 8, 11, 12, 15, 16, 17, 21, 22, 23, 24, 29, 31, 35, 36, 37, 48, 49, 50, 51, 52, 53, 54, 57, 63, 64, 71, 76, 82, 85, 88, 91, 92, 98, 104, 109, 110, 117, 119, 120, 127, 132
Stimulate, 18
stories, 20, 26, 71
story, 6, 26, 27, 40, 116, 117, 121
subconscious mind, 2, 3, 108, 139

suggestions, 7, 11, 14, 17, 19, 20, 23, 38, 71, 85, 92, 93, 95, 97, 108, 110, 120, 124, 127
suspend, 9, 19, 85, 107, 123, 131, 133
tangible, 9, 27, 28, 42, 90, 116, 124, 126
task, 13, 16
teaching, 2, 3, 7
techniques, 1, 2, 3, 17, 21, 69, 71, 120
The Secret, 2, 25
Theta, 7
Thinking Patterns, 15
thoughts, 14, 18, 19, 22, 23, 27, 28, 29, 30, 31, 32, 34, 35, 36, 37, 40, 42, 44, 52, 53, 54, 62, 63, 71, 74, 82, 92, 93, 103, 104, 105, 107, 108, 117, 121
trance, 6, 7, 18, 71, 93, 108, 120, 138
Ultradian rhythms, 6
unconscious, 2, 3, 4, 5, 8, 23, 92, 108
unconscious mind, 2, 3, 4, 108
value, 1, 18, 20, 21, 32, 42, 43, 63, 66, 67, 69, 72, 73, 80, 81, 82, 84, 89, 92, 103, 104, 116, 132
Values, 15
want, 1, 2, 3, 7, 8, 9, 12, 13, 14, 15, 18, 19, 21, 23, 24, 25, 26, 32, 33, 34, 35, 36, 37, 38, 39, 40, 41, 42, 43, 44, 47, 48, 49, 50, 52, 56, 57, 59, 61, 72, 74, 76, 79, 80, 82, 85, 88, 89, 90, 91, 92, 93, 95, 96, 98, 99, 104, 105, 106, 108, 109, 110, 111, 112, 113, 114, 115, 117, 118, 119, 120, 121, 123, 124, 125, 127, 128, 132, 133, 134, 137, 138
wealthy, 19, 20, 32, 89, 90, 97, 99, 134
wishful-thinking, 7
zone-out, 11

THE AUTHOR BRYAN WESTRA

The Law of Hypnosis has brought me much success and happiness. I wrote this book that you might benefit in the same way from this law as I have.

Naturally, I can't teach everything I've learnt in one book alone. Please take a minute to learn more by visiting:
www.indirectknowledge.com

Learn Well! Live Well!

Bryan James Westra

www.ingramcontent.com/pod-product-compliance
Lightning Source LLC
Chambersburg PA
CBHW032027230426
43671CB00005B/225